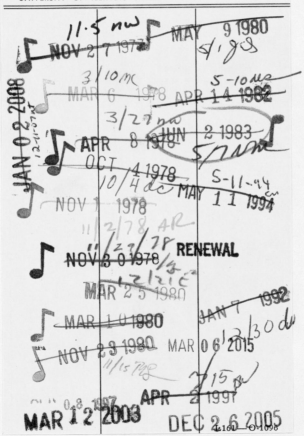

REVOLUTION
IN
SOUND

REVOLUTION IN SOUND

A Biography of the Recording Industry

by C. A. Schicke

Illustrated with photographs

LITTLE, BROWN AND COMPANY
Boston   Toronto

FIRST EDITION

T 06/74

Library of Congress Cataloging in Publication Data

Schicke, Charles A
  Revolution in sound.

  1. Phonorecords--Industry and trade. I. Title.
ML3790.S34   338.4'7'789912   74-2459
ISBN 0-316-77333-6

Published simultaneously in Canada
by Little, Brown & Company (Canada) Limited

PRINTED IN THE UNITED STATES OF AMERICA

To the memory of
Ted Wallerstein

Edward Wallerstein

Preface

In 1972, Americans, most of them teen-agers and young adults, spent more than $1,800,000,000 on records and prerecorded tapes, an amount exceeding what they spent at motion picture box offices. During the past ten years the recording industry has consistently proven that it is among the most important of the mass entertainment media, a position it had held back in the days before radio, talking pictures and television. Yet despite the immense popularity of records and tapes, few people know very much about how recordings are made, or how artists and songwriters make money, or how the industry evolved; very little has been written about the subject.

Members of the business community have long viewed the recording business as a strange, twilight world alien to all other kinds of businesses. To some extent this impression is justified. The industry has throughout its history been populated by charlatans, counterfeiters, unscrupulous speculators and other shady characters. But it has also enjoyed more than a generous share of great showmen, brilliant scientists, superb creative artists and dedicated businessmen of vision and high purpose. In truth, it is a business that must conform to the basic laws of economics just like any other business, although it is certainly far more exciting and absorbing than most.

The intent of this book is to describe the events that led to the industry's high status; and to outline how a modern recording company functions in relationship to its employees, its artists and its public.

Contents

ix

Contents

PART ONE

A Brief History of Recorded Sound

1

The Cylinder Turns

THE BIRTH of recorded sound was announced with little fanfare. The columns of the December 22, 1877, edition of the *Scientific American* reported in a straightforward manner that a machine capable of capturing and reproducing natural sounds was a reality. The inventor of the remarkable device, Thomas Alva Edison, called it the "phonograph." However, more frequently he referred to the machine as "my baby."

Edison was only thirty years old at the time, but the former telegraph operator from Michigan was already a familiar figure to the staff of the magazine. He had made invaluable contributions to the budding communications industry. Of particular importance was his solution to the problem of harmonic telegraphy. Now several messages could be sent over the same telegraph wire in either direction simultaneously. His perfected stock market ticker was a godsend to Wall Street brokers. The patents for these and other inventions had established the young inventor

A drawing of Edison's original phonograph as it appeared in Scientific American, *December 22, 1877*

as a scientific genius of the first rank and had brought him considerable wealth. But Edison, never one to accumulate money for the mere sake of having it, promptly poured the income he made from the sale of his patents into various research projects he was conducting at his new laboratory in Menlo Park, New Jersey. One of the first of these projects to be completed successfully was the phonograph that he carted to New York to show off at the *Scientific American.*

Under the watchful eyes of a few staff members, Edison placed a strange-looking cylindrical contraption on the editor's desk. After a few seconds' pause, he began turning a handle attached to the right end of the cylinder and suddenly, according to an eyewitness account, "The machine inquired as to our health, asked us how we liked the phonograph, informed us that *it* was very well, and bid us a cordial goodnight. These remarks were not only perfectly audible to ourselves, but to a dozen or more persons gathered around."

The reaction of the small audience was electric. Within a few minutes, news of the miraculous gadget spread like a brush fire through the offices and out onto the cobblestoned streets of lower Manhattan. From seemingly nowhere, a crowd sprang up, jamming the halls and the staircase of the building. Everyone pressed and strained to hear the machine that talked. The editor, fearing that the weight of the crowd would cause the staircase to collapse, regretfully asked Edison to stop the demonstration. From that point in history, nearly a century ago, recorded sound was launched on its erratic but always colorful way.

By current standards, the first model of the phonograph seems like a toy; but in the context of its day, it was a masterpiece of mechanical ingenuity.

Edison had made up the word "phonograph" from two shorter words of Greek origin: "phono," meaning sound or voice; and "graph," meaning written or recorded. Along with its descendants for almost the next fifty years, the phonograph was an acoustical, or sound-powered, machine.

By the nineteenth century, scientists knew a great deal about the physical properties of sound. They were aware that the source of any sound is a vibrating body that sets surrounding particles of air, gas or water in motion. These particles strike a second group of particles, which in turn strikes a third group, and so on. Meanwhile, after striking the second group, the first group bounces back only to collide again with the vibrating body. Thus the whole process is started over again. Since the second and third groups also bounce back and recollide, sound energy is transmitted back and forth, in wavelike motions. Each time the particles make contact, energy is expended; so, as the particles are pushed outward from the source, the force, or amplitude, of the sound is lessened.

Sound would not mean much to us if we did not have ears equipped to receive it. Our middle ears consist of membranes called eardrums, which are caused to vibrate by the particles as they are pushed outward from the source of the sound. As the eardrums' vibrations move in sympathy with those generated by the source of the sound, they trigger a relay of nerve signals to the brain, where the sound is identified and its location gauged. Several factors help the brain to determine this information, among them: the frequency of the sound (the number of vibrations per second); the strength, or amplitude, of the particles set in motion by the sound as they strike the surface of our eardrums; and the interval, or difference in time, at which the sound waves reach each ear.

In 1857, a French physicist, Leon Scott de Martinville, built a machine that functioned somewhat like the human ear called the phonautograph, to measure the amplitude of different kinds of sounds. When the machine operated, a megaphone collected sound waves from the source being measured. They, in turn, caused a membrane, or "diaphragm," stretched across its narrow end to vibrate. A bristle attached to the diaphragm transmitted the vibrations onto a sheet of a black paper enfolding a large, cylindrical drum that was rotated by a handle. These wavelike tracings were exactly in step with the sound waves collected by the megaphone. Thus they provided accurate measurements of the force of sound generated.

Edison's first phonograph bore a resemblance to Scott's laboratory instrument, but Edison, whom his co-workers had affectionately nicknamed "the Professor," reasoned that a diaphragm-driven stylus, or needle, might do much more than merely scratch sound waves on black paper. Why could it not transcribe actual sounds onto some suitable soft surface? According to his own account, he had come to this conclusion while conducting his experiments on harmonic telegraphy:

> My own experiments that this [the recording of sound] could be done came to me almost accidentally while I was busy with experiments, having a different object in view. I was engaged upon a machine intended to repeat Morse characters, which were recorded on paper by indentations that transferred their message to another circuit automatically, when passing under a tracing point connected with a circuit-closing apparatus.
>
> In manipulating this paper, I found that when the indented paper was turned with great swiftness, it gave off a humming sound resembling human talk heard indistinctly.
>
> This led me to try fitting a diaphragm to the machine. I saw at once that the problem of registering

human speech so that it could be repeated by mechanical means as often as might be desired, was solved.

Indeed, Edison had miraculously "solved" the problem. John Kreusi, an aid at the Menlo Park laboratory, built a prototype of the phonograph from Edison's sketches in the fall of 1877. It was a much smaller machine than the cumbersome phonautograph. Instead of a bristle, Kreusi used a metal stylus, which he attached to a sturdy diaphragm made of mica. The diaphragm was in turn secured to the bottom of a horn, sometimes called a resonator. In place of the drum, Edison's specifications called for a small brass cylinder, the entire surface of which was engraved with a continuous spiral groove. The cylinder was mounted on a hand-rotated, screwlike metal rod. The actual recording surface — Edison called it a "phonogram" — was a thin sheet of tinfoil that wrapped around the cylinder.

To make a recording, the operator cranked the handle of the machine, which moved the cylinder laterally, while someone spoke, sang, or played a musical instrument into the recording horn. The sounds collected by the horn caused the enclosed diaphragm to vibrate in an up-and-down motion, thus driving the attached stylus in and out of the surface of the tinfoil like a trip-hammer, forming thousands of tiny dents. To re-create the original sounds, the process was simply reversed. The stylus of the playback unit was set at the beginning of the series of dents, which fitted in the continuous groove on the engraved surface of the cylinder. The cylinder was then set in motion; and as the playback stylus retraced the course of the recording stylus, falling in and out of the dents, it

Original tinfoil phonograph

caused the attached diaphragm to vibrate in a way almost identical to the way that the recording horn diaphragm had vibrated during the recording phase. The playback unit horn amplified the re-created sounds generated by the diaphragm so that they were clearly audible to the listener.

The early models of the phonograph featured separate recording and playback units. In later years the two functions were combined in one unit.

It was a simple and rather obvious idea, but no one except Edison had made it work. As a matter of fact, even he was amazed at the ease with which he had accomplished his goal. In later years, he recalled his reaction to hearing the first recording ever made, his own reading of "Mary Had a Little Lamb": "I was never so taken aback in my life. I was always afraid of things that worked for the first time."

As soon as Edison's accomplishment became public, an

absolute mania over the phonograph sprang up. Edison was hailed as the greatest living inventor. Of course, Edison's success depended to a great extent on the theories and speculations of the other great scientific minds of his century.* But in the late 1870s, when the Industrial Revolution was in full stride, the practical man was king. Certainly Edison, who had risen from humble newsboy to world renowned scientist, was the epitome of the era, and the public lionized him. They flocked to Menlo Park where "the Professor" seemed never to tire of entertaining his visitors with the full gamut of tricks he could play on the phonograph. The machine could sneeze, weep, cough, wheeze or talk in many languages. The delighted visitors were usually surprised to discover that the man who had made this great contribution to the science of sound was obviously hard of hearing.

In April 1878, Edison carefully packed up a model of his "baby" and journeyed to Washington, D.C., to put on a series of demonstrations. The first of these was held at the Smithsonian Institution in the presence of the great American scientist Joseph Henry. Later, the phonograph played to spellbound audiences in the White House and the Capitol Building, as well as in England and France.

Meanwhile, the American business establishment was already in motion. Gardner Hubbard, a lawyer who

---

* Oddly, about two months before the first public announcement of the phonograph, an article in a French scientific periodical reported that a man named Charles Cros had written a paper describing a machine with capabilities similar to those of Edison's phonograph. Later investigation was to prove that Cros had never done much more than theorize about his machine. A working model was never built. And although a great deal has been written about the incident, no one, not even Edison's most severe critics, has ever been able to prove any connection between the two developments.

founded the National Geographic Society and was Alexander Graham Bell's father-in-law, formed a syndicate of investors who bargained successfully with Edison for the right to manufacture and sell models of the phonograph. Thus was formed the Edison Speaking Phonograph Company. The company was operating by the middle of 1878. But the question now was how to make money with the miraculous gadget. The most obvious way, of course, was to exploit its tremendous novelty appeal. James Redpath, a lecture tour expert, was hired to organize nationwide exhibitions. He quickly recruited a group of enterprising men with a flair for showmanship. They were first subjected to a training course in the care and maintenance of the phonograph. Then they were introduced to the mysterious art of making tinfoil phonograms, a far from easy task. It took a lot of practice to make phonograms that produced sounds that were at least recognizable. At the conclusion of the instruction period, Redpath's men were turned loose on an eager public.

The phonograph was an immediate sensation. Crowds crammed lecture halls, theaters, vaudeville houses and exhibition tents to see and hear Edison's marvelous machine put through its paces. Redpath's men rapidly hit upon the successful ploy of inviting members of the audience to participate in the diverting exercise of making phonograms. Very often, local musicians were invited onstage to record "live" before the audience. These guest artists were almost always virtuosos on the trumpet, cornet or trombone, because the touring representatives of the Edison Speaking Phonograph Company learned very early in the game that the machine reproduced the powerful sounds of brass instruments particularly well.

But the event that always brought down the house was

a demonstration of pitch changes. By altering the speed at which the cylinder was turned, the operator could make a basso sound like a soprano in a split second. This trick completely captivated the crowds and convinced thousands of satisfied customers that the phonograph was good, clean fun for the whole family.

While the "baby" was the star attraction on the sawdust trail, Edison, in a reflective mood, wrote down ten serious objectives for his favorite invention:

1. Letter writing and all kinds of dictation without the aid of a stenographer.
2. Phonographic books that will speak to the blind without effort on their part.
3. The teaching of elocution.
4. The reproduction of music.
5. The "Family Record" — a registry of sayings, reminiscences, etc., by members of a family in their own voices, and of words of dying persons.
6. Music boxes and toys.
7. Clocks that would announce in articulate speech the time for going home, going to meals, etc.
8. The preservation of language by exact reproduction of the manner of pronouncing.
9. Educational purposes; such as the preserving of the explanations made by a teacher, so that the pupil can refer to them at any moment, and spelling or other lessons placed upon the phonograph for convenience in committing to memory.
10. Connection with the telephone, so as to make that instrument an auxiliary in the transmission of permanent and invaluable records, instead of

being the recipient of momentary and fleeting communications.

All of Edison's more practical objectives were to be achieved, with an assist some years later from the tape recorder. But at the time he wrote out the list, he was practical enough to realize that none of them would ever be achieved unless he greatly improved the phonograph. And for the better part of 1878, he directed his almost inexhaustible mental and physical energies to that end.

It was not an easy task. The shortcomings of his machine were many and not easily resolved. The tinfoil phonogram played for only a minute or so; and it wore out after only five or six playings. Then there was the serious problem of trying to replay a phonogram once it had been removed from the cylinder. It was almost impossible to realign the tracings on the tinfoil with the grooves of the cylinder. Human speech, though recognizable, was far from distinct; the *s* sound was completely lost. Another serious drawback was the necessity of driving the machine by hand.

Edison's experiments toward solving these problems were numerous and wide-ranging. One line of experimentation led to the design of a disc phonograph resembling our modern stereo turntables. But he decided to drop this approach when he discovered that the sound increasingly deteriorated as the playback stylus neared the center of the flat tinfoil disc. As the distance actually covered by the stylus was shortened with each revolution of the machine, the stylus traveled at steadily decreasing rates of speed toward the center. The slower the speed, the less efficiently it functioned. The result was a breaking up of the recorded sound, which today we call distortion. Edison also found that it was difficult to maintain accurate pitch at lower speeds.

These problems continue to plague record manufacturers in the present; and they were to influence greatly Edison's course of action in the record industry for many years to come.

Edison also experimented with a variety of hand-wound, spring-powered motors and different types of semisoft materials, in the hope of finding a suitable replacement for the harsh, metallic-sounding tinfoil phonogram.

Six months passed without a significant breakthrough, and as time wore on, Edison's mind became increasingly occupied with thoughts of a new project — the development of a practical electric light. This ambitious undertaking involved far more than the development of a long-burning incandescent lamp. Huge generators of a type never before dreamed of had to be designed and constructed to provide electrical power to cities and rural areas. And factories capable of mass-producing inexpensive electric light bulbs would have to be planned, constructed, and staffed. Edison was to accomplish all three objectives at the cost of ten long years of constant mental and physical labor.

By the latter part of 1878, his involvement with the electric light was so all-consuming that he scarcely gave any thought to his "baby." When a newspaper reporter asked him if he had made any further progress on the phonograph, Edison dismissed the subject curtly, stating that the invention was "a mere toy with no commercial value."

Edison had turned his back on the phonograph at a particularly bad time for the future of the machine. The public's interest in the miraculous machine was fading rapidly. Audiences in exhibition halls and county fair tents were dwindling. There was no doubt about it; the novelty of the phonograph had worn off. Since there was no practical use for the apparatus, the Edison Speaking Phonograph Company was forced to shut down. During its brief life span, it had manufactured only five hundred phonographs.

Now completely absorbed in his new mission, Edison bought controlling interest in the dormant company, with no apparent thought of reviving it. He probably did have some vague plan to return to the further development of the phonograph when time permitted, but meanwhile it was to be placed on the shelf. He seems to have felt that no one else would dare to take up the cause of recorded sound in the interim. Not only did he believe that his patents on the machine were foolproof, but he also felt confident that the worldwide acclaim he had received for the invention clearly attested to the fact that recorded sound was his private endeavor. If that was his attitude, time seemed to bear it out. For the following eight years, the matter was pigeonholed. Or so Thomas Edison believed.

2

The Graphophone

IF EDISON was complacent about his "baby," this attitude was undoubtedly shattered during a reported visit in May of 1886 by two representatives of the Bell Laboratory. Bell was an institution dedicated to electrical and acoustical research that Alexander Graham Bell, inventor of the telephone, had established some years before. According to the account of Alfred O. Tate, Edison's secretary, the Bell ambassadors told Edison that two of the laboratory's researchers, Charles Sumner Tainter, a highly skilled technician, and Chichester Bell, a chemical engineer and an English relative of Alexander Graham Bell, had just been granted several patents for devices to improve the phonograph. These devices, the Bell emissaries stated, were incorporated into a new talking machine called the graphophone.

This new apparatus was the culmination of five years of intensive research and experimentation inspired by Alexander Graham Bell's unflagging interest in the potential of Edison's phonograph.

The graphophone, as it was described to Edison, closely resembled the phonograph in physical appearance, but it differed from the old machine in several significant ways. The tinfoil phonogram had been replaced by a wax-coated cardboard tube that slipped onto the metal cylinder. The soft wax surface not only permitted finer grooving, thereby extending the playing time of the machine, but it also eliminated the harsh, grating sounds of the tinfoil. However, there was a drawback. Although the sound of wax cylinders was certainly smoother, better defined and more pleasing, it was considerably lower in volume than the sound generated by the old phonogram. This necessitated the addition to the machine of stethoscopic ear tubes to further amplify the sound level.

The major difference between the graphophone and the phonograph was in the methods they used to transcribe sound onto the actual recording surface — whether tinfoil or wax. The rigid metal stylus of Edison's phonograph made vertical indentations on the tinfoil phonogram as it traced the groovings of the brass cylinder. The graphophone, on the other hand, featured a loosely mounted stylus that cut hill-and-dale grooves directly into the wax-coated cardboard. The playback stylus of the graphophone rode smoothly in the grooves, rather than in the herky-jerky manner of the phonograph. This so-called floating stylus did much to improve the quality of playback sound.

According to Tate, the Bell envoys proposed to Edison that a partnership be formed, and they offered to underwrite the cost of all future development. But Edison rejected the offer without hesitation. He felt, perhaps justifiably, that they had violated his basic rights. But his rather testy response was probably mostly due to his recent falling-out with his backers in the electric light enterprise. Doggedly insisting on the use of direct current rather than alternating current for long-distance power transmission, he had clung to this position in the face of mounting evidence that he was wrong. Still smarting from this experience, he was certainly not about to let anyone share in the rewards to be gleaned from an improved talking machine.

Spurred by the threat of the graphophone, Edison immediately set to work again on the phonograph. His strategy was to make a better machine than the graphophone, regardless of the possibility of infringing on the Tainter-Bell patents.

The old Edison Speaking Phonograph Company was reorganized as the Edison Phonograph Company at the inventor's new headquarters in West Orange, New Jersey. For the better part of the next two years, the "baby" was again uppermost in his mind.

The phonograph was no longer to be a toy or a vaudeville diversion. But what should be its function? Edison decided to concentrate on the number-one item on his old list of objectives for the phonograph — the "crude toy" was to become an office dictation machine.

Before long, a foot treadle similar to those used for propelling the sewing machines of the era and a battery-driven motor became optional replacements for the irksome hand crank. The motor sported a flywheel governor that guaranteed that the cylinder would rotate at a constant speed.

Edison also proceeded to improve some of the devices patented by Tainter and Bell. The weight of the floating stylus — now a sapphire needle — was so reduced that

Thomas Edison with an early battery-driven model of the phonograph

the depth of the hill-and-dale grooves that it cut was only 1/1000 of an inch. He developed a phonogram made entirely of wax to replace Tainter and Bell's wax-coated cardboard tube, the advantage being that the solid wax cylinder could be shaved and reused repeatedly, thereby enhancing its value for office use. The new phonograph also featured a so-called spectacle device, which combined the recording stylus unit and the playback stylus unit in such a way that they could be easily interchanged. This made it possible for the operator of the machine to check on what had been recorded very quickly.

Edison made certain that his progress was reported to the enemy camp. The press was continually bombarded with news of the latest developments. Meanwhile, both Chichester Bell and Charles Tainter decided that the time was ripe to sell their patents. These were purchased by a group of Washington investors led by a particularly shrewd businessman by the name of Colonel Payne. The syndicate, which included a United States Supreme Court reporter named Edward D. Easton, formed the American Graphophone Company, and persuaded Tainter to join the staff.

The backers of the new venture were extremely anxious to protect their investment, which was imperiled by competition from Edison. They decided to promote the graphophone as an office dictating machine powered by foot treadles or battery-driven motors. The members of the syndicate were keenly aware that they had a distinct advantage in being located in the District of Columbia, where thousands of government offices would provide an immensely fertile market for their equipment. The company began manufacturing graphophones at a former sewing machine factory in Bridgeport, Connecticut, and graphophone salesmen were soon soliciting orders from business and government office managers. Edison, at the moment, was still tooling up to launch his new phonograph. But the graphophone had a considerable head start.

However, Colonel Payne was not the sort of man who could be content merely with winning a skirmish in a commercial war. He and his colleagues began to plot a legal attack against Edison, accusing him of infringements of the Tainter and Bell patents. And as the early sales returns began to come in to American Graphophone, it looked as though the court fight might yield the greater profit. Sales were well below expectations; and the future of the graphophone did not appear promising. But the looming

legal contest was averted, at least for the time being, by
the arrival on the scene of Jesse H. Lippincott.

The 1880s were years in American history when monop-
olists and trust builders flourished. Federal laws prevent-
ing the formation of monopolies and cartels to eliminate
competition and to rig prices were still several years in
the future. Lippincott, a true son of his age, was a dedicated monopolist. By 1888 he had amassed a fortune in
the glass tumbler business. Restlessly in search of new
worlds to conquer, he decided at the suggestion of a
friend to gain control of the talking machine industry
while it was still in its infancy and the stakes were comparatively low. He discovered that to accomplish this end
he would have to make deals with both Edison and Colonel Payne.

Edison, now middle-aged and constantly in need of
cash to finance his research projects, came to terms rather
quickly. He sold Lippincott his talking machine patents
and exclusive sales rights to the phonograph for $750,000,
though he wisely reserved manufacturing rights to the
machine. The money was to be paid to Edison in install-
ments by Lippincott's newly formed North American
Phonograph Company.

Colonel Payne proved to be a much harder man to
deal with at the bargaining table, despite the fact that
the American Graphophone Company was deeply in trouble. Payne retained manufacturing rights to the graphophone, and he refused to sell Lippincott the Tainter-Bell
patents. He did, however, with one notable exception,
agree to sell national sales rights for $200,000, but grudg-
ingly, and only after Lippincott guaranteed that he would
buy thousands of machines every year. The exception was

a sales territory encompassing the District of Columbia, Delaware and Virginia that had already been franchised to Edward D. Easton and a group of Washington businessmen. Payne also refused to deal directly with the North American Phonograph Company; he insisted that the pact be made with Lippincott personally. This arrangement was to have important consequences in years to come.

Soon after the ink dried on the contracts, the North American Phonograph Company began to make plans to market both the phonograph and the graphophone. Lippincott decided to copy the sales policies of the fast-growing Bell Telephone Company, even though the two businesses were not at all similar. He divided the country into geographical territories, and began to license exclusive exploitation rights to the machines to local companies within these areas. The machines handled by the local companies were not to be sold; they were to be rented for a fee of forty dollars a year, with North American and the local companies sharing the rental income. It was far from an ideal arrangement, but it was probably the only course open to Lippincott in view of the fact that the machines were very expensive and few customers could have afforded to buy them outright.

Within a year, thirty-three companies were licensed. Most of them assumed the names of the states or areas in which they operated: the Ohio Phonograph Company, the Pacific Phonograph Company and so on. Edward D. Easton and his partners from American Graphophone obtained sales rights to the graphophone and Edison's phonograph for Virginia, Delaware and the District of Columbia. Following the practice of the day, they named their organization the Columbia Phonograph Company, and thus the oldest trademark in the record industry was established. It is worth mentioning here for reasons we will come to later that Easton also continued to be a stock-holder in the American Graphophone Company.

Despite the golden hopes of a monopolistic future, Lippincott's empire began to crumble almost from the day it was conceived. Sales were awful. Harried equipment salesmen found that government and business office stenographers — almost always men in those days — fought tenaciously against the acceptance of the machines. The stenographers considered them menaces that threatened their livelihoods. The machines themselves were expensive and generally unreliable. Matters were made worse when customers discovered that spare parts for the two machines were not interchangeable. Even the size of the wax recording cylinders differed. By early 1891, after two years of operation, the total number of machines in circulation was only three thousand. And of that number, the better engineered phonograph had outsold the graphophone by a ratio of 50 to 1. This poor showing diminished the ranks of the local companies. Of the original thirty-three, only nineteen survived. Lippincott, watching his empire sink into a quagmire of troubles, became a sick and disheartened man, unable to meet his obligations to either Edison or Colonel Payne. Edison must have shared Lippincott's despondency. It certainly looked as though the phonograph had failed for the second time, and that it was doomed once more to gather dust on the shelf.

But this was not to be the fate of recorded sound. In a matter of a few short months, the once dying business was to be transformed into a thriving industry with limitless prospects for the future. The man who was to make all this possible is one of the truly unsung heroes of his time. Today his name, Louis Glass, appears only in small type or in the footnotes of out-of-print books about phonograph records.

3

The Nickel-in-the-Slot Saves the Day

LOUIS GLASS was the manager of the Pacific Phonograph Company in San Francisco. In 1889 he became convinced that his franchise would most certainly go under if it were to continue relying on the office rental business for its existence. At that time, penny arcades and amusement centers featuring coin-operated mechanical games and musical instruments were springing up all over the country. Glass was struck by the notion that the public might just be willing to pay money to hear a cylinder machine play. With this in mind, he designed an ingenious mechanism that automatically opened and closed an electrical circuit between the storage battery and the motor of an Edison phonograph. When a nickel was deposited in a slot on the machine, the motor started the cylinder of the machine rotating, and subsequently stopped it. Glass also equipped his special machine with four sets of listening tubes. The deposit of a nickel put the machine in motion and opened one set of tubes; each of the additional sets

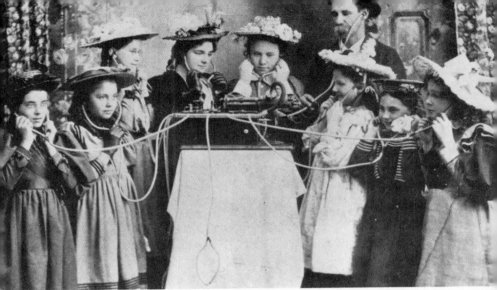

Stethoscopic ear tubes were needed to amplify the sound produced by early cylinder machines

of tubes could be opened by depositing an additional nickel. The experimental machine, therefore, could earn from five to twenty cents for each play of an "entertainment cylinder."

Glass installed the equipment in the Palais Royal Saloon in San Francisco and soon patrons there began dropping nickels in its slots with great enthusiasm. Glass did not waste any time. Within another year he had installed pay phonographs in eighteen other locations.

At about this time, Felix Gottschalk, the manager of the Metropolitan Phonograph Company in New York City, also began to consider the possibilities of the coin-operated phonograph. The two men met in 1890, with the result that Gottschalk bought Louis Glass's patents and subsequently formed the Automatic Phonograph Company. Soon after, Gottschalk began to sell coin mechanisms and multitube listening attachments to the local companies of the North American Phonograph family. Gottschalk found that he was, happily, in a seller's market. The struggling local companies were willing to try almost anything to keep their foundering franchises afloat, even if it meant sacrificing their legitimate office machine rental businesses on the tawdry altar of the amusement trade. Hundreds of coin-operated phonographs and graphophones were placed in saloons, amusement parks, ice cream parlors, drugstores, penny arcades and numerous other establishments. The public was captivated and delighted with its new mechanical toy. The coin-operated cylinder machine was an immediate nationwide success. The nickel-in-the-slot had saved the day for recorded sound.

As the number of pay locations increased, so did the demand for "entertainment" cylinders. North American, the local companies, and the two manufacturing companies — Edison, and American Graphophone — made plans to record and sell prerecorded cylinders to coin machine operators. The fact that the cylinders played for only two minutes or so, and that the quality of the sound was downright awful, did nothing to dampen the public's enthusiasm.

The Columbia Phonograph Company quickly established itself as the leader in the field of making entertainment cylinders of good quality. It must have been an alert and enterprising organization, for before the end of 1891, it had published a ten-page catalogue of prerecorded cylinders featuring selections by the great bandmaster and composer John Philip Sousa and the United States Marine Band. Another artist featured prominently was John Y. Atlee, the superb whistling virtuoso, whose lilting renditions of "The Mockingbird" and "Home Sweet Home" were eagerly sought by coin machine operators for their choicest pay locations.

The North American Phonograph Company announced that it would begin to issue "original" cylinder recordings by artists of an exceptionally high caliber. These included the great cornetist Jules Levey, tenors Ed Francis and Will Nankerville, baritone Ed Clarence and piccolo soloist R. K. Franklin.

This was a rather unusual practice for that time, because most of the musicians and singers who made recordings received no credit on cylinder labels or in catalogues. In fact, the record catalogues of the early nineties did little more than list titles under general descriptive headings such as "Sentimental," "Topical," "Comic," "Irish" and "Negro."

This practice was to continue for many years, despite the fact that it was both unfair to the artists and inadequate for the needs of a growing business — for as the number of coin-machine locations mushroomed and nickel-spending fans multiplied, it became apparent that the distinctive sound and style of certain artists attracted more nickels than others; and the recording star system was born. John Philip Sousa and the United States Marine Band were perennial favorites. George H. Diamond's recordings of "You Will Never Know a Mother's Love Again" and "Have One On the Landlord With Me" were in great demand, and established the singer as a star. Tenors William F. Denny and George J. Gasken became famous for their interpretations of sentimental love ballads. Len Spencer and George W. Johnson were noted specialists at recording Negro songs. Johnson was certainly unusual in that racially insensitive era when Negroes were jokingly referred to as "coons." He actually was black. His first hit was "The Whistling Coon."

Talking recordings were also quite the rage, particularly those that offered stories about Irish comic characters. There were stories by a fictional character named Pat Brady, performed in a thick brogue by a veteran actor, Dan Kelly. But Pat Brady was soon outstripped by a new Irish character called Michael O'Casey. The O'Casey stories were created by a young actor named Russell Hunting; and they were to become by far the most popular of their type. Hunting became so successful at making recordings that he later abandoned the theater for a career in the record industry, advancing gradually from producer to high-level executive over a period of thirty years.

As the cylinders of the nineties ground out the tinny-sounding music of the brass bands and the tearful ballads of the music hall tenors, one man dedicated himself to elevating recorded sound to a higher status. Signor Gianni Bettini, a wealthy ex-cavalry officer and Parisian boulevardier of Italian origin, foresaw that the phonograph could be a preserver of his favorite art form, grand opera. Bettini managed to acquire an Edison phonograph at a time when, technically, they were being leased rather than sold. He spent a great deal of time tinkering with the machine to see if he could improve upon it. The result of his experiments was a device called the micro-reproducer, which he patented in 1889. It consisted of a recording stylus mounted on a number of metal legs that were embedded in a mica diaphragm. This device was nicknamed "the spider." The numerous legs were supposed to transmit more accurately the vibrations of the diaphragm to the stylus and vice versa. The result, Bettini contended, was "perfect" sound, and he persuaded many leading opera stars of the day to record on his machine.

From the practical standpoint, Bettini seemed to be wasting his time. There was literally no market for his recorded cylinders. Certainly opera recordings could not compete with the stories of Pat Brady and Michael O'Casey at the coin machine locations; and machines were still leased, rather than sold. Occasionally someone did manage to buy equipment outright, as Bettini had, but the price was prohibitive except for the wealthy few. Nevertheless, Bettini worked seriously at improving his recording techniques, perhaps with the foreknowledge that recordings would one day become a popular form of home entertainment.

This was not a fruitless exercise. The production of cylinder recordings was at best an inexact science, improved upon only through constant practice and much trial and error. Recording engineers and producers guarded their hard-won secrets jealously. The human voice presented the greatest challenge because very few voices reproduced well on acoustical recordings. The timbre of the voice chosen to record was of paramount importance. Other key factors in making a clear vocal recording were diction, enunciation and the angle at which the voice was projected into the recording horn.

At a typical recording session of the early nineties, a singer or speaker faced a bank of three battery-motored phonographs. (Electricity was now available from Edison's giant generators, but it was considered too unreli-

An early acoustical recording session. Note that the rear of the piano, with its back removed, faces a recording horn

Actress Sarah Bernhardt making a master cylinder record

able for recording sessions.) A brass band, with its far greater sound generating capacity, accommodated ten machines. Before each recorded performance, convention dictated that a studio aide or the artist go to each machine, start it, announce the name of the selection into the recording horn, and stop it. When the actual performance began, all of the machines were started simultaneously. Since the number of duplicates that could be made from an original cylinder was small, this process was repeated over and over until the singers and musicians collapsed from exhaustion. The record companies encouraged the performers to stick it out as long as possible by paying them a fixed fee for each recorded performance, or "round," as they were called. The top stars received about five dollars per round. Artist royalties were not even dreamed of at the time.

Duplicates of the master cylinders made at recording sessions were manufactured by the pantograph method, a crude and inefficient way of transferring sound from one cylinder to another. The stylus of the machine used to play back the master cylinder was connected by a metal rod to the cutting stylus of a second, or "slave," machine. When the machines were set in motion, the sound vibrations captured in the grooves of the master cylinder were transmitted through the metal rod to the cutting stylus and into the surface of the duplicate cylinder. It was not a satisfactory process because the soft wax master cylinder deteriorated with each successive playback. A master cylinder was rarely capable of producing more than twenty-five duplicate cylinders of quality. The other great drawback of the pantograph method was its simplicity. It made copying easy. Coin machine operators soon discovered that it was cheaper to make their own pantograph duplicates of hit cylinder recordings than to buy additional copies.

Nevertheless, as the mid-nineties approached, the Columbia Phonograph Company continued to lead all rivals in "best-selling" cylinder recordings. Sales, mostly derived from mail orders, climbed to an average of 350 units per day. The official price was fifty cents a cylinder — or five dollars for a dozen — but coin machine operators were willing to pay much more for particularly clear popular recordings.

Ironically, Louis Glass's nickel-in-the-slot machine saved the record business from probable extinction, but it did nothing to solve the staggering problems confronting Jesse Lippincott and his North American Phonograph Company. The pay machine war touched off a commercial battle that virtually destroyed Lippincott's small monopoly. Opportunistic machine shop operators, defying the patent laws, flooded the marketplace with illegally manufactured machines and accessories at bargain prices. Record pirates enjoyed a brisk trade in copies of popular cylinders. These equipment counterfeiters and the record pirates diverted from Lippincott the revenue he desperately needed to fulfill his commitments and sustain his faltering organization.

Edison suggested that a substantial reduction in the price of cylinders would discourage the record pirates. He believed this could be accomplished by tooling up for a new mass-manufacturing process he had just developed; but neither he nor Lippincott had the capital to finance the project.

The situation steadily grew worse. By 1893, it was

known in the trade that not one graphophone had been manufactured in two years and that Lippincott had not been able to pay Edison for the phonographs he had purchased during that period. It was also generally known that he had made only token payments on the $750,000 he had promised Edison in return for patent and sales rights to the phonograph.

Lippincott's death threw the problems of the little industry into bold relief. Edison, North American's chief creditor, made the first move. He persuaded Thomas Lombard, the company's new president, to drop the cumbersome practice of leasing machines rather than selling them outright. Under the new policy, the local companies were to function as sales representatives only.

Edison's new plan was proposed at the National Phonograph Convention of 1893. His keynote address to the delegates from the twenty-two existing local companies was delivered on a high note of optimism: "I will yet live to see the day when phonographs will be almost as common in homes as pianos and organs are today."

The home entertainment potential of the phonograph appeared to be the only ray of hope left to the North American Phonograph Company. The delegates, recognizing that fact, accepted Edison's new plan. There was one exception: the Columbia Phonograph Company had other ideas.

Columbia's Edward D. Easton also recognized the possibility that the home entertainment market held enormous promise. But why attempt to tap this potential within the debt-ridden framework of the North American organization? Why not go it alone? Easton had all the necessary facilities. By shrewd stock transfers and manipulations, he and his associates had acquired control of the American Graphophone Company with its idle factory but still valuable Tainter-Bell patents. Since Colonel Payne had made American Graphophone's original contract with Lippincott personally, Easton was able to wriggle free of the North American complex rather easily.

This was not true for Edison, who became hopelessly enmeshed in North American's many serious problems. He and his advisors eventually concluded that the only course of action left was to regain direct control of his phonograph patents and start all over again. To accomplish this end, Edison, as chief creditor, threw the North American Company into bankruptcy after assuming the company's liabilities. The resultant claims by creditors and disputed settlements brought a rash of legal suits and countersuits which tied Edison up in court entanglements for two solid years. During this time he was prohibited by court orders from manufacturing either machines or cylinder recordings.

He used the time well. He established a foothold in Great Britain, where he was free of legal restraint; and he designed an efficient spring-driven motor to drive the phonograph. But most important, in 1895 he began building the foundations of the National Phonograph Company, a new organization that would sell machines and cylinder records.

Meanwhile, the new Columbia–American Graphophone combine took full advantage of its head start. The fortunes of the two firms and their ownerships became so closely interwoven from this point on that we can refer to them as one company, namely, Columbia.

Once free of the North American complex, Columbia's

first order of business was to take up where it had left off when Jesse Lippincott appeared on the scene: suit was brought against Edison for infringements of the Tainter-Bell patents. Columbia also brought suit against most of the local companies in the North American family on more or less the same charges. This systematic legal campaign was so successful that virtually all of Columbia's competitors in the production of commercial cylinder recordings were eliminated. Edison, on the other hand, was to prove a more formidable opponent in the courts.

Columbia was fortunate to have in its employ a brilliant Scotch engineer, Thomas Hood MacDonald, who developed an inexpensive, dependable, hand-wound spring motor for the graphophone. In 1894 Columbia introduced the revolutionary new machine to the market at a retail price of only eighty dollars, roughly half the cost of the old office machines. Recorded sound was now within the reach of prosperous Americans, and they bought it.

Within two years Easton had organized a broad network of dealers and distributors to sell machines and recordings to the home market. In 1896, a new illustrated catalogue listing thousands of recorded titles was published; and a new model of the graphophone selling for only fifty dollars was unveiled.

That same year, Edison finally freed himself from his legal entanglements and began to put the final touches on his own new company. Columbia was now to have some competition.

The future of the cylinder record business seemed assured. Graphophones had been readily accepted in front parlors and sitting rooms, and the prospect of healthy competition between Columbia and Edison

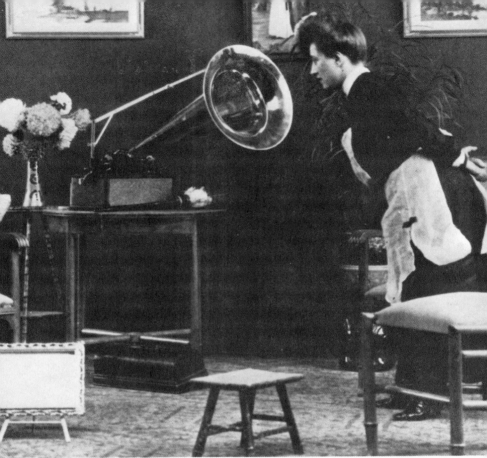

The cylinder phonograph in a front parlor typical of the 1890s

brought the promise of higher quality and lower prices.

But the record business has never been fated to enjoy either stability or standardization for very long. The earliest and one of the most dramatic instances of that fact was the appearance of the Berliner Gramophone Company, an organization dedicated to the proposition that flat discs were superior to cylinders.

4

The Whirling Disc

ALTHOUGH the inventor of the new flat record had been on the scene for some time and had made no secret of his activities, both the Edison and the Columbia camps had ignored him. Undoubtedly, they were convinced that his invention was a mere toy. This proved to be a serious miscalculation.

Emile Berliner had come to the United States from Germany in 1870, when he was nineteen years old. During the next few years, as he wandered from job to job, he pored over books on chemistry and physics, eventually developing a particular interest in electrical and acoustical research.

One of Berliner's first accomplishments was the design for an improved telephone transmitter. He sold the rights to the transmitter to the Bell Company and shortly thereafter accepted a research job at the Bell Laboratory. Later, he quit his job with Bell and began to concentrate his energies on independent acoustical research.

Emile Berliner

*The first disc talking machine or gramophone, exhibited
by Emile Berliner in 1888*

As he proceeded with his experiments, he became intrigued by the possibilities of the flat disc recording. He was undoubtedly aware that both Scott, the inventor of the phonautograph, and Edison had pursued these possibilities before him, and that he would never be able to obtain strong patent rights to a disc machine. However, he concluded that if he could develop a new method of cutting grooves into the surface of discs, he would be able to obtain unassailable patent rights to the process. A substitute would have to be found for the hill-and-dale method of incising grooves used both by the graphophone and the phonograph. The solution, he thought, lay in the phonautograph's zigzagging, laterally cut grooves.

Berliner soon developed a chemical process for preparing wax-coated zinc discs. During the recording phase, the stylus cut its groove tracings through the wax coating and onto the zinc surface. The disc was then dipped in a chromic acid bath. The acid ate into the tracings left by the recording stylus, forming permanent grooves of the desired depth and width.

The first chemically made zinc records were harsh and grating and often produced a severe surface hiss; but the "level," or volume, of sound produced was much higher than that produced by cylinders. The reason for this was quite simple. The energy required to cut hill-and-dale grooves into the hard wax surface of the cylinder was supplied solely by acoustical power. The thin wax coating on the surface of Berliner's zinc disc offered very little resistance to the lateral movements of the cutting stylus, so far more energy was applied directly to the formation of the grooves. Furthermore, the chemical reaction of the acid supplied additional energy to the whole process.

Thus even the first crude gramophone machines — as Berliner called his disc playback apparatus — required only a reproducing horn, whereas the cylinder machine required stethoscopic ear tubes.

By 1888, although Berliner had not been able to come up with a satisfactory method of reproducing his metal discs, he apparently did feel confident enough to demonstrate the gramophone and his discs before members of the Franklin Institute in Philadelphia that year.

After playing his machine, Berliner proceeded to make several predictions to his audience. He told them that he envisioned a day when he would be able to produce thousands of copies of his original zinc discs. He further prophesied that great performers would earn royalty payments derived from the sale of copies of their original recordings. But most important, Berliner foresaw the gramophone and the disc as a home entertainment and educational medium that would be used on a grand scale.

It must be remembered that in 1888 Berliner's already established competition still thought of the phonograph and the graphophone as "talking machines." The fact that cylinders could be made by anyone, and duplicated pantographically anywhere, was considered a strong selling point by those who marketed the machines as office dictation devices. Unlike Berliner, they failed to see the mass entertainment possibilities of recordings.

Eventually, Berliner conceived of a relatively inexpensive method of reproducing copies from his original zinc discs. Reverse, or "negative," discs were produced by means of an improved electrotyping process. These negatives, or "stampers," were in turn pressed into heat-softened hard rubber biscuits. Once the rubber biscuit cooled and hardened, it was an exact copy, or "record," of the zinc original.

Finally, in 1893, Berliner felt he was ready to launch his revolutionary machine commercially in the United States. He formed the patent-holding United States Gramophone Company, and a year later a distributing company was organized for the purpose of manufacturing and selling gramophone machines and records. However, Berliner and his associates lacked sufficient capital to exploit their new products, and they made little headway during the first two years. Prospective investors found it difficult to take the new-fangled talking machine very seriously. Although it was much cheaper than the established cylinder machines — selling for only twelve dollars — it had several faults, the most glaring of which was the necessity of propelling the machine by hand.

Today, one of the first commercial models of the gramophone is on exhibit at the Smithsonian Institution. It looks like an extremely primitive forerunner of a modern stereo turntable. Its basic components are few and highly functional. A free-swinging wooden arm is attached to the side of the turntable platform. The playback unit is mounted on the top of the free end of the wooden arm. The unit consists of a metal stylus connected to a reproducer, or sound box, that is in turn linked to a small conical horn made of metal for increased amplification.

In its day, the gramophone played hard rubber records measuring seven inches in diameter, with a playing time of approximately two minutes. They could be bought locally in Washington for fifty cents each, or five dollars for a dozen.

The operation of the early gramophone required the

body control of a practiced contortionist. With one hand the operator had to crank the turntable until he estimated that it was spinning at 70 revolutions per minute. He then placed the needle in the outer groove of the disc with his free hand, while still cranking away with the other. This exercise could hardly have been considered a relaxing form of home entertainment.

Once Berliner actually became involved in the business of making disc records he found that he needed someone to act as a recording director and talent scout. In 1894 he persuaded a young Columbia Phonograph Company producer named Fred Gaisberg to take the job. Gaisberg had to rely for the most part on nondescript local talent, including musicians and singers recruited at a local Indian medicine show. Besides these unknown performers, Gaisberg persuaded the great balladeer George J. Gasken and the monologist Russell Hunting to record in the new medium. As was the custom of the day, they were given no credit on record labels.

Early in 1895, Berliner's company was issuing new disc records on a regular basis. Later that year a group of Philadelphia businessmen bought a block of Berliner's stock for twenty-five thousand dollars, and the new enterprise finally had the capital it so desperately needed.

5

The War Between
the Disc and the Cylinder

THE ESTABLISHED graphophone and phonograph companies paid little attention to Berliner and his raucous-sounding gramophone. They were far too busy battling one another.

Columbia was prospering with MacDonald's spring-motored graphophones. But Edison's entry into the field in 1896 with a forty-dollar spring-motored model of the phonograph posed a serious threat. Columbia met Edison's thrust in two ways: by introducing the twenty-five-dollar Columbia Graphophone, and by bringing yet another legal suit against Edison. The battle dragged on in the courts for months without resolution. Both sides finally decided to close the case when they realized that time was running out on their patent protections.

Two years later, in 1898, Edison was finally in a position to compete with Columbia effectively. His superbly engineered Home Phonograph, which retailed for only twenty-five dollars, was an immediate and overwhelming success. Yet even with this triumph, Edison was never quite able to surpass his arch rivals.

But by this time it scarcely seemed to matter. From 1896 to 1898, the cylinder record and equipment business flourished for everyone. The greatly reduced cost of players and the vast improvements made in amplifying horns and in recording studio techniques stimulated a wave of consumer buying. And although phonographs and graphophones were fast becoming sitting room fixtures throughout the nation, commercial phonograph parlors, now equipped with spring-driven coin machines, continued to prosper and grow in number.

After twenty years, the recording industry at last began to fulfill its earlier promise. The leading recording artists of the late nineties were becoming international celebrities. Russell Hunting's well-recorded stories "Casey as Judge," "The Dying Soldier" and "The Steamboat" kept him in the forefront of the most popular recording stars. Dan Kelly and his "Pat Brady" stories was not far behind, nor were William F. Denny, "a tenor of pure tone and much pathos," and the ever-popular George J. Gasken or Dan Quinn, who specialized in musical comedy songs.

As record sales soared, smaller companies were encouraged to compete with the major firms. Reed and Dawson of Newark claimed to have produced the only successful violin recording, with T. Herbert Reed. The Norcross Phonograph Company of New York City promoted recordings of potpourris from Italian opera. But the only serious opera recordings of the era were produced by Gianni Bettini soon after players were installed in the households of well-to-do Americans. Bettini established a steady mail-order trade in high-priced opera and drama cylinder records. In 1897, he was offering his select clientele songs by the immortals Yvette Guilbert and Nellie Melba; recitations by Mark Twain and Sarah Bernhardt; and arias by various Metropolitan Opera stars. But no recording company, large or small, could challenge the Columbia artist roster. Russell Hunting, Dan Quinn, George J. Gasken, Steve Porter, piccolo soloist George Schweinfest, banjo virtuoso Vess L. Ossman and the mighty Sousa Concert Band were only a few of the great stars in the most powerful array of recording talent hitherto assembled in one company's catalogue.

The recording boom of the middle and late nineties was not confined to the United States. The Pathé Brothers of Paris soon boasted the largest phonograph salon in the world — a huge pay-as-you-listen establishment employing forty people. In 1896, the company began to make recordings with local opera and comic opera stars for the diversion of salon customers as well as for the growing number of cylinder record buyers. Three years later, Pathé published a catalogue listing fifteen hundred titles. In Great Britain, Edison and Columbia representatives squared off for a long fight for market dominance that was finally resolved by a merger in 1898. To a lesser degree, the recording boom spread to Germany, where a few small companies sprang up, and to Italy, where phonograph parlors modeled on the Pathé salon flourished for a time.

As the century drew to a close, it appeared that Edison's fortunes were finally on the upswing, and that he would at last reap some much-deserved rewards from his favorite invention. The sturdy Edison Home Phonograph had become a staple in the equipment market, and Edi-

IT
TALKS
FOR
ITSELF

"They didn't have anything like this when I was young"

Write
for
Catalogue
No. 91

THE GRAPHOPHONE

ALL THE GRAPHOPHONE ASKS IS A HEARING.

Matchless for home entertainment. It reproduces musical and other records clearly and brilliantly. On Graphophone cylinders one can make records of music, the human voice, or any sound, and reproduce them at once. Other so-called talking machines reproduce only records made in laboratories.

COLUMBIA PHONOGRAPH CO., Dept. 91.

New York, 143 and 145 Broadway.
Retail Branch, 1155, 1157, 1159 Broadway.
St. Louis, 720-722 Olive St.
Philadelphia, 1032 Chestnut St.
Washington, 919 Pennsylvania Ave.

Chicago, 211 State St.
Paris, 34 Boulevard des Italiens.
Baltimore, 110 E. Baltimore St.
Buffalo, 313 Main St.
San Francisco, 723 Market St.

COURTESY CBS RECORDS

An advertisement from 1898 of the cylinder graphophone, emphasizing its home entertainment attractions son cylinder records were beginning to sell well, particularly in the rural areas of the country where the Professor's name was sheer magic.

The real issue of the time, however, was not whether Edison or Columbia would ultimately triumph in the fight for leadership, but which form of record would win out — cylinder or disc.

The gramophone forces made enormous technical and organizational progress during the closing years of the century. Berliner had designed a spring-motored model of the gramophone player that was greatly improved upon by a machine shop operator named Eldridge P. Johnson from Camden, New Jersey. The Berliner Gramophone Company contracted with Johnson to manufacture the hand-wound players, and by late 1897 he was turning them out by the hundreds. The twenty-five-dollar price of the disc machine was competitive with the graphophone and the phonograph. Another significant advance was the substitution of shellac pressings for the warp-prone rubber discs.

Berliner had great talents as an organizer, in addition to his obvious technical gifts. In 1896 he established the National Gramophone Company to distribute players and disc records. Among the young company's staff members were Frank Seamon and William Barry Owen.

Seamon, an aggressive, promotion-minded salesman, quickly took charge of the domestic operation; and his consistent, forceful and hard-hitting advertising campaigns soon made the gramophone a household word throughout the country.

In 1897 Owen sailed for London to found the Gramophone Company Ltd., the European branch of the Ber-

Eldridge R. Johnson in 1900

A spring-motored model of the gramophone

Eldridge Johnson's machine shop in Camden, New Jersey, where the first spring-motored gramophones were manufactured

liner Gramophone dynasty. Within a year, he had raised enough capital to open an office and to import machines and records from the United States. By the end of 1898, Owen had sold every gramophone player he had imported. His success was due to two factors: he used Seamon's proven hard-hitting promotional tactics and, more important, he had fertile ground in which to work, since the cylinder machine had not yet — with the exception of the Pathé dynasty in France — put down strong roots in Europe.

Owen's astonishing success spurred plans at the Gramophone Company Ltd. for immediate expansion. It was decided that the importation of records and machines was too slow a process to keep pace with the demands of a rapidly growing business. In Germany, Emile Berliner's brother Joseph was assigned the task of building a record pressing factory and a plant to assemble gramophone players from parts shipped from the United States. Fred Gaisberg and his brother Will were dispatched to London to set up a recording studio operation for Owen.

Soon after the Gaisbergs became established in London, they began to make frequent trips to the music capitals of Europe to record the leading grand opera stars of the era. In three short years the gramophone had become an important factor in the record industry throughout the world.

Obviously, to have achieved such spectacular success, the gramophone disc must have offered certain practical advantages over the cylinder recording; and it did. The disc produced far greater levels of sound than those produced by cylinder machines, and therefore did not require the use of the onerous ear tube. The disc was also easier to carry around, and it took up less storage space than the cylinder. Of little consequence as far as the public was concerned, but of prime importance from a business standpoint, was the fact that the disc could not be pirated.

In spite of the obvious advantages of the gramophone, Columbia became convinced that the market was ripe for a cylinder machine capable of greater sound volume. Accordingly, in 1898 the company introduced the Graphophone Grand. This huge machine, designed to play a jumbo-sized wax cylinder, had greatly increased sound generating capabilities. Where before stethoscopic listening tubes had been required, now a large horn sufficed. The one-hundred-fifty-dollar price tag that the machine carried made it too costly for any but the affluent. Nevertheless, Edison felt compelled to join in the folly by producing a competitive model (at one hundred twenty-five dollars) called the Edison Concert Phonograph.

Neither cylinder machine made much of an impact on the public. This is not surprising, considering that the equally loud Improved Gramophone, an elaborate and sturdy player designed by Eldridge Johnson, sold for only twenty-five dollars, and that fifty gramophone discs could be stored in the same space required to store one concert-sized cylinder.

As time went on, the two major cylinder companies at last came to the realization that the gramophone was a threat to their very existence. Berliner, Johnson and Seamon clearly had a great economic advantage in being able to mass-produce and sell records that were virtually impossible to pirate. The old pantograph copying mechanism, like the modern tape recorder, encouraged widespread counterfeiting of cylinder records. This was costing cylinder record producers thousands of dollars in lost sales revenues. So, the ever-aggressive and enterprising Columbia Phonograph Company decided to take positive action.

In an era when companies rushed to the courtroom at the slightest provocation, Columbia was no exception. The company's attorney, Philip Mauro, was an extremely clever man and more than a match for anyone else in the legal business. Mauro attacked the Berliner organization at its most vulnerable spot. His brilliantly organized and persuasive suit was not directed at Berliner's patent-controlling United States Gramophone Company. Instead, he launched a campaign against Seamon's sales agency, the National Gramophone Company, on the grounds that the firm had infringed upon the Tainter-Bell floating stylus patent of 1886. Mauro knew that this ploy, if successful, would halt the sales and distribution of equipment and records nationally. It would then be senseless for Berliner to continue to operate his manufacturing facilities.

In 1899, the courts ruled in favor of Mauro's brief, and an order was issued restraining Seamon from operating. Seamon immediately countered with an appeal to a higher court, and succeeded in having the restraining order put aside pending a thorough hearing of the case.

Sometime later, for reasons that are unclear to this day, Seamon suddenly reversed his position and became a bitter foe of his own business colleague, Emile Berliner. Seamon may have inferred from Mauro's success that Berliner's patents were not as unassailable as they once had appeared to be and that there was now a great opportunity to challenge Berliner. The rewards of victory would surely be a share in the profits of the flourishing disc machine and record business. On the other hand, Seamon's defection may have been prompted by his dissatisfaction with the profits his agency earned from the sale of gramophones. Whatever his motivation, Seamon reorganized the National Gramophone Company into the National Gramophone Corporation and shifted his base of operations from New York City to Yonkers, New York.

The evidence seems to indicate that Seamon, at this point still reluctant to challenge Berliner's patent rights directly, helped to manufacture disc machines and records surreptitiously. Berliner became suspicious of these maneuvers and stopped all shipments of machines and records to the new agency. Seamon's products were advertised under the Vitaphone trademark later that year.

Berliner was quick to claim infringements of his patents. But before he could organize his defense, Seamon, perhaps feeling more confident, boldly announced that his agency was offering for sale a revolutionary new disc machine called the Zonophone. Actually, the Zonophone was almost an exact copy of the Improved Gramophone.

There is good reason to suspect that Seamon's confidence was inspired by a secret pact he had made with Columbia. This seems to be borne out by his testimony before the court of appeals to the effect that in his opinion Berliner had indeed violated the Tainter-Bell floating stylus patent. He then accepted Mauro's injunction against the National Gramophone Company. Of course, this was an empty gesture, since he had already dissolved that company. But the court nevertheless agreed with Seamon's arguments and those advanced by Mauro. It ordered Berliner not to manufacture gramophones without the express consent of the owner of the Tainter-Bell patent, namely, Columbia.

It is most probable that Columbia's real interest in the affair was to gain access to the rapidly expanding disc machine and record business. Inhibiting the competition posed by the gramophone was very likely only a secondary consideration. The favorable court decision brought matters out in the open. Seamon signed a formal contract with Columbia, granting the company sole rights to manufacture the Zonophone. In return, Seamon was to receive royalties and full patent protection.

Naturally, Emile Berliner and his associates fought back with countersuits brought against Frank Seamon. The upshot of all the legal haggling was that the booming American disc business ground to a sudden halt. A lasting result was that the term "gramophone," which had become the subject of this bitter legal controversy, was never again used as a record player trademark in the United States.*

Meanwhile, Eldridge Johnson was the victim of prosperity. In the midst of the hostilities, he found himself in possession of an enormous inventory of machines and a greatly expanded manufacturing facility. Since his creditors were getting restless and since he was not directly involved in the suits brought against Berliner, he decided to go it alone. In 1899, he formed the Consolidated Talk-

---

* The term "gramophone" did, however, gain a solid foothold in Europe, where it applies to any disc record player to this day. In the United States, the word "phonograph" drifted back into the lexicon as a term encompassing all record players, even though it originally applied only to Edison's cylinder machine.

ing Machine Company as a vehicle to sell machines and records directly to the public. With a great flourish, he announced a "marvellous" improvement in the art of making records.

During his association with Berliner's company, Johnson gradually had come to the realization that the sound of the gramophone disc itself would have to be improved if further development of the playback equipment were to be significant. In 1896, he had secretly set out to find a method superior to Berliner's zinc disc process. He finally hit on wax recording blanks, coated thinly with graphite for the conduction of electric current.

The Improved Records, as Johnson named them, were an unqualified success. Orders poured into Johnson's Philadelphia headquarters for the new discs, which offered recorded performances by Sousa's Concert Band and the Metropolitan Orchestra, represented by such popular titles as "Koonville Koonlets," "Smoky Mokes," "The Irish Swell Waltz," "The Girl in the Barracks" and "The Mandalay Two-Step." Vocalists too were well represented. Basso George Broderick was featured in a number of titles, including "Father O'Flynn" and the "Turnkey's Song" from *Rob Roy*. A vocalist named S. H. Dudley offered "Father Won't You Speak to Sister Mary" and "Nancy" (with whistling chorus). Among the great Dan Quinn's contributions were "The Mick Who Threw the Brick" and "Pletty Little Chinee from 'San Toy.'" Arthur Collins and E. M. Favor were heard in "Cindy, I Dreams About You," "I Ain't Seen No Messenger Boy," "My Honey Lou" and "other coon songs." But the two most prominently displayed selections in the Improved Record catalogue were performed by the Haydn Quartet:

A Trip to the Country Fair (Describes the railroad
journey, noise of train, side show barkers and
fakirs. The inevitable hand organ is present. A
very catchy number.)

Farmyard Medleys: both a medley and a melody.
Combined with the sweet music of the singers
are the familiar barnyard noises. Roosters crow-
ing, dogs barking, cows mewing, and hens cack-
ling. A delightful reminder of summer days on
the farm.

6

The Disc Wins Out

IN MARCH of 1901, Frank Seamon, still locked in his legal battle with Berliner, asked for a court injunction to prevent Johnson from selling gramophone machines. But this time the irrepressible Seamon was defeated. Johnson's sound, carefully prepared defense of his position won out, and he was permitted by the court to continue operating. Not long after, Seamon and Mauro suffered another blow: the injunctions against Berliner were lifted. In October, Johnson and Berliner formed a new firm called the Victor Talking Machine Company. Berliner and his associates received 40 percent of the common stock in the new company in exchange for the gramophone patents; Johnson received most of the remainder of the stock in return for his contribution to the new organization, the flourishing Eldridge R. Johnson plant in Camden.

Johnson, a fervent believer in advertising, launched the new company on its way with a massive campaign. It was during this period that Victor Records introduced the special trademark that was to become the most famous symbol in the record industry throughout the world — the picture of the dog "Little Nipper" listening to an Improved Gramophone under the caption "His Master's Voice." From 1901 on, Johnson had Little Nipper's portrait printed on all Victor record labels.

The picture was a copy of an original painting by Francis Barraud that had been purchased by William Barry Owen in London for one hundred pounds (about five hundred dollars in 1901) and sent as a gift to Johnson and Berliner. Owen could well afford the gesture. Sales of gramophone players and records were skyrocketing in the United Kingdom and throughout continental Europe. The great prosperity of the Gramophone Company Ltd. and other Victor affiliates on the Continent provided a great stimulus to the production of new recorded material. The 1901 edition of the Gramophone Company catalogue featured songs and arias in every European language and many Oriental languages.

At the suggestion of a retail store owner in Saint Petersburg, the Russian branch of the Gramophone Company began recording the stars of the Imperial Opera, among them a sensational young basso named Feodor Chaliapin. These disc records, like all others at this point in history, were one-sided, and they sold for the equivalent of five dollars, an exorbitant price in those days. To distinguish them from regularly priced records, they were issued under a special red-colored label. Despite their high price, they were an immediate success. Soon most of the other Gramophone organizations in Europe were busily releasing expensive "Red Seal" recordings by opera celebrities, and Eldridge Johnson began importing them into the United States with considerable success.

Francis Barraud's painting, "Little Nipper," which became the trademark of Victor Records

A model of a disc graphophone player with tone arm

At about this time Johnson made one of his greatest contributions to the development of record playback equipment — the tone arm. This device shifted the weight of the sound box and the horn from the surface of the record to the frame of the machine itself. Thus the playing life of the gramophone record was considerably extended.

The booming sales of Victor's disc players and records finally led both Edison and Columbia to mass-produce

60

wax cylinder records in 1901. But this concerted effort to establish the cylinder on the same commercial footing as the disc came far too late to alter the inexorable course of history. The disc had already won the battle. Although cylinder sales increased at a modest pace while disc sales were booming, Edison remained imperturbable. He was convinced that the disc would always be acoustically inferior to the cylinder because of the deterioration of sound in the inner grooves.

Columbia, on the other hand, had no such doubts about the disc. Easton viewed its worldwide success with considerable envy. Columbia's previous attempt to enter the disc field via the Zonophone had ended in a maze of legal entanglements and a court-enforced cessation. But now, by a quirk of fate, Columbia was about to be able to have a foot in both the disc and the cylinder camps.

Columbia's passport to the disc business was provided by a young man named Joseph Jones. Some four years earlier, Jones had worked as a summer employee in Berliner's laboratory, doing odd jobs and running errands. During this time he had witnessed Berliner's experiments with wax recording blanks. Neither Berliner nor Johnson, later, had dared to apply for a patent for the process of cutting grooves onto the surface of wax recording blanks, for fear of violating the Tainter-Bell patents owned by Columbia. But their concerns had little effect on Joe Jones, who decided to write a set of specifications and apply for a patent on the process himself. To his own surprise and everyone else's, the patent office granted him a patent in 1902. It was to be revoked nine years later, but that development came too late to affect the next chain of events.

Columbia's quick-witted Philip Mauro lost no time in

buying the patent rights from Jones for an enormous sum for those days, twenty-five thousand dollars. Now, with the Jones patent safely in his pocket, Mauro was convinced that Columbia had an ironclad right to manufacture disc machines and records. By the early part of 1902, three models of the new Columbia disc graphophone player appeared on the market at popular prices, ranging from fifteen dollars to thirty dollars. Seven-inch discs were offered at the standard price of fifty cents each. Ten-inch discs sold for a dollar.

The disc graphophone was almost an exact copy of the machine manufactured by Victor and, consequently, Eldridge Johnson promptly threatened to bring legal action against Mauro and his principals. Of course, Mauro had the Jones patent as his ace in the hole. As no one concerned wanted to undergo another tiresome series of legal suits, the two parties settled out of court. Johnson was awarded the assets of Seamon's former Zonophone empire. In exchange, he provided Columbia with technical information. From this point on, Victor and Columbia were to pool all such information, making the two companies the dominant forces in the record business for decades to come.

Once the legal squabbling ended, the record companies began to focus their attention on making better records and machines in an attempt to capture a bigger share of the constantly growing market.

The next competitive arena became the opera house. It is difficult for us, living in a multimedia communications age, to adequately appreciate the true status of the opera stars of the early twentieth century. They were international celebrities perched on the highest rung of the entertainment ladder. Their names were household words even among people who hated opera music.

This phenomenon was reflected in the immediate public acceptance of the few Red Seal records that Johnson imported in 1902. Encouraged, he made plans to begin his own ambitious Red Seal recording program with Metropolitan Opera stars. But before he was able to get the program under way, he was preempted by his rival at Columbia, Edward Easton. In 1903, Columbia announced with great fanfare the release of its Grand Opera Series, on disc only. Some think that Easton chose disc over cylinder for the series because the disc had by now been established as the recording vehicle of the middle and upper classes who listened to opera.

The Grand Opera Series, featuring arias by Ernestine Schumann-Heink, Edouard de Rezke, Antonio Scotti and other opera notables of the day, was hurriedly prepared for exhibition at the St. Louis World's Fair. But in spite of all the hoopla, the venture ended in failure, perhaps because the public did not associate Columbia — until now a cylinder company exclusively — with grand opera disc recordings. Victor Records had cornered that market.

Meanwhile, Johnson did not wait for the completion of his domestic Red Label recording program to launch the new series on Victor. Under a program that he arranged with Owen, in 1903 Johnson began manufacturing Red Seal records produced abroad. Within the year Victor sales were brisk. In September, the recorded performances from abroad were supplemented with records produced by C. G. Childs in Victor's Carnegie Hall studios, featuring the great stars of the Metropolitan Opera: the great American mezzo-soprano Louise Homer, and

Enrico Caruso recording for Victor Records
(a self-caricature)

Antonio Scotti and Johanna Gadski. In January of 1904, the sensational young Italian tenor Enrico Caruso was engaged to sing in New York. He was promptly signed to a contract by Childs.

Up to this point, musical artists had been paid flat, or one-time, fees for their work in the studio. Thus it had been customary for grand opera singers to drift from studio to studio, recording for anyone who could pay their fees. Childs realized that to persuade the stars to record for Victor exclusively, he would have to offer them the opportunity of sharing in the success of their records. This he accomplished by establishing a system of royalties, whereby an artist would be paid a percentage of the money earned on each copy of his record sold. Years would pass before the artist royalty concept would spread to rival record companies or infiltrate the popular recording field; but Childs's system was the first evidence that the prophecy made by Emile Berliner at the Franklin Institute in 1888 would be fulfilled.

It was roughly from this point on that the industry was to enjoy what has been referred to as "the golden age of records." The record player, whether a disc or a cylinder machine, was now the most popular form of home entertainment. Opera stars would go on to earn millions of dollars in royalties on record sales.

One of the events that paved the way to the golden era occurred in Europe. An American named F. M. Prescott, who had originally been associated with Frank Seamon, established a new record company in Paris called the International Talking Machine Company. His record label was named Odeon, after a favorite theater in Paris. Odeon discs differed from all previous discs in one important respect: they offered recordings on both sides. Before long, this revolutionary feature swept across Europe and became firmly implanted in the United States.

Eldridge Johnson made yet another major contribution to the industry in 1906, when he introduced a new gramophone machine called the Victrola. The impact of this new player was phenomenal. It was to make such an indelible mark on the public's consciousness that for many years following, the name Victrola was commonly applied to any phonograph, regardless of its actual brand name.

The Victrola offered two sensational new features. The recording playback horn, which had been for many people a dust-gathering eyesore, was now enclosed within the body of the Victrola. The turntable and the tone arm, previously exposed, were now hidden under the lid of the machine. The four-foot-high Victrola was the first console record player; it looked like a piece of furniture. The audio buffs of the day complained that the sound pro-

COLUMBIA
DOUBLE~DISC RECORDS

MUSIC ON BOTH SIDES

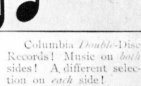

Columbia *Double*-Disc Records! Music on *both* sides! A different selection on *each* side!

And *both* for 65 cents—practically the price of *one*—32½ cents for each selection! They may be played on *any disc machine*, no matter what make, and they give you *double value for your money*, plain as daylight—better surface, better tone and far greater durability. If you have not heard a Columbia Record issued during the last year and a half, don't say that you know what your talking machine can do. The present Columbia process of recording produces a *naturalness* and *roundness* and *perfection* of tone that is positively unequalled in any other. Send 65 cents for a sample and a catalog and the name of our dealer.

Columbia *Double*-Disc Records! Double discs, double quality, double value, double wear, double everything except price! Don't put your record money into any other!

COLUMBIA PHONOGRAPH CO., Gen'l, Box 215, Tribune Bldg., N.Y.

Columbia's advertisement illustrating a major innovation
after the turn of the century — the two-sided disc

Evolution of Victor's Model XI
1910-1926
The most Popular Victrola

1,049,198 WERE MADE,
ALL CONSOLES EXCEPT 6,392

1917
$110.⁰⁰
List

1910
$100.⁰⁰
List

1922
*(No.100)**
$150.⁰⁰
List

1912
$100.⁰⁰
List

1923
*(No.100)**
$150.⁰⁰
List

* Catalog number changed from XI to 100

Early twentieth century models of the Victrola, the most popular record player of the acoustical era

duced by the downward-pointing internal horn was not on a par with the sound of the external horn, but the public paid no heed. There was little sales resistance among those who could afford the two hundred dollar price.

By the middle of the first decade of the twentieth century, the disc had distinctly succeeded in capturing the buying power of the upper and middle classes and the

67

urban populations. The cylinder's stronghold — and mostly Edison cylinders at that — was the poorer, rural market.

Edison's distributors and dealers relied heavily on mail-order sales. They invariably pushed the sale of Edison cylinders and players on a "cash or easy payment" basis following a "free trial" period. The accompanying literature usually emphasized Edison's "rags-to-riches" life story, and his long list of inventions. Impressive catalogues were printed in the tens of thousands. However, almost none of the listings in these catalogues were accompanied by artist credits, even at this relatively late date. Record numbers and titles were followed by the briefest description. For example, "Flanagan on the Farm" is described as a "talking sketch"; "Kentucky Babe" is sung by a "Vassar Girls' quartette," whoever they might have been. "A Lemon in the Garden of Love" is followed by the terse message, "Big hit song."

But Edison obviously knew his market. In 1907, he enjoyed his greatest business year since entering the phonograph industry. Sales for equipment and records totalled $7,000,000. This was a great deal of money at a time when a dollar bill bought a meal in the most expensive restaurant in the country.

But the success of the cylinder was destined to ebb. A severe depression struck the United States and Europe late in 1907. Both the cylinder and the disc businesses suffered, but the less firmly entrenched cylinder trade was far less able to withstand the shock. The slump forced Edison to shut down his European operations, except for an occasional recording session in England or on the Continent.

Unfortunately for Edison, the slump came just at a time when he finally felt he could compete successfully with the disc business. He had just introduced the Edison Amberola Phonograph, his answer to the highly popular Victrola. It was a large machine with the capability of playing jumbo-sized cylinder records, each lasting four minutes. As with the Victrola, the recording horn of the new machine was completely enclosed. The price tags of the Victrola and the Amberola were identical — two hundred dollars.

Bolstered by his new high-priced phonograph, Edison set out to compete with Victor for the carriage trade. He began issuing four-minute Amberola cylinders featuring some of the great opera stars of the day. Anticipating the documentary potentials of the recording medium, he persuaded William Jennings Bryan and William Howard Taft, the presidential candidates in 1908, to record their campaign speeches for posterity.

Though Edison persisted in his cylinder business, no other company thought it worthwhile to continue. Columbia announced to its dealers in 1912 that it was closing down all phases of its cylinder trade. Yet in that same year, Edison, at sixty-five, repledged his faith in cylinders with the announcement of a revolutionary new celluloid record called the Blue Amberola. Record historians maintain that this cylinder record was the crowning achievement of the acoustical recording era. The hard, smooth surfaces of the Blue Amberola eliminated the annoying hissing sounds common to the surfaces of all other types of records of the day. The hill-and-dale method used in cutting its grooves also contributed to its acoustical superiority. During a typical disc recording session, engineers often had to hold the studio musicians down to prevent the laterally moving recording stylus from breaking the walls of the grooves during particularly loud passages. This was not a concern at a hill-and-dale cylinder session, since the recording stylus did not move from side to side. The louder the passage, the more deeply the stylus cut into the recording blank surface, with no effect on the groove walls.

Although Edison was clearly still committed to the cylinder, he had known for some time that he would have to enter the disc business out of economic necessity. But he was determined to enter it in a different way than Berliner. In 1912 he announced the creation of the Diamond Disc Phonograph and the Diamond Disc Record. It came as no surprise to anyone at the time that Edison elected to cut his new discs by the hill-and-dale method.

Finally embarked on the disc business, Edison was also the only existing producer of cylinder records left in the world. And he was not about to disappoint the millions of owners of still-operable cylinder machines. Despite a steadily dwindling demand for cylinder records, Edison was to cling to his self-imposed obligation to manufacture them for seventeen more years.

7

The Height of the Golden Age

DURING the period immediately preceding the outbreak of World War I, records, particularly disc records, became a genuine cultural force. The center of opera recording activity gradually shifted from Europe to the United States. Attracted by generous fees and royalties, the grand opera luminaries of the era flocked to the New York City studios of the well-endowed Victor Talking Machine Company.

The Gramophone Company Ltd., Victor's European affiliate, did not resent the fact that the center of opera recording had shifted to the United States. The company retained exclusive distribution rights to the new American operatic recordings in Europe and the rest of the world, with practically no capital investment required. Therefore, records issued on Gramophone's His Master's Voice label (HMV) continued to be available at relatively little cost. More important, Victor's preoccupation with opera allowed the British firm's engineering staff to concentrate on the improvement of orchestral and instrumental recording techniques.

Their experiments yielded notable results. The 1913 edition of the HMV catalogue listed new records featuring several great violinists, including Pablo Sarasate, Fritz Kreisler and Mischa Elman, and performances of Beethoven's Leonore Overture No. 3, Grieg's *Peer Gynt Suite* and Schubert's *Unfinished Symphony*. These recordings represented historic innovations in the field of recorded music. Their existence demonstrated that European recording engineers had solved a number of serious acoustical recording problems — the greatest of which had been the difficulty of capturing the delicate sounds of the stringed instrument family.

For years, record companies had skirted this problem by issuing brass band transcriptions of orchestral pieces, whether classical or popular. The enormous volume capacities of brass and percussion instruments had been ideally suited to the recording facilities of the day, but of course they had not been able to approach the subtle sound of the violin with its soft overtones.

It is said that necessity is the mother of invention. The studio men of the early 1900s proved it. At recording sessions, members of the studio orchestra were placed on platforms of various heights and at various distances from the recording horn. The louder members of the brass family were placed farthest from the horn. The bell of the overpowering tuba was faced away from the horn; the tuba player used a mirror to follow the conductor's baton. The gentle instruments — the flute, the oboe, the violin and the viola — were placed very close to the recording horn. Violinists used an instrument specifically designed for acoustical studio use called a stroh-violin. This weird instrument featured a special attachment consisting of a diaphragm and a horn, which worked together to amplify the sounds generated by the violin itself and to focus them accurately at the recording horn. Yet even with stroh instruments, violin players were still forced to cluster together to avoid being overwhelmed by the sounds emanating from the other sections of the orchestra. The violin's big brothers, the double bass and the cello, fared much worse. They were rarely used in the studio at all, since it was virtually impossible to capture lower string registers on wax recording blanks — or on cylinders, for that matter. Cello and double bass parts in an orchestral score were substituted for by brass instruments or the deeper woodwinds.

All of the sounds generated by studio musicians were funneled via the recording horn into the mysterious recording room, the carefully guarded bastion of the recording engineer. Visitors, or even friendly musicians, were rarely permitted to enter this inner sanctum, although, according to one eyewitness, there was actually little to see: a turntable, some extra diaphragms, and a small oven to render the wax recording blanks soft enough for groove cutting.

The studio orchestras of the day, even those engaged for the recording of large-scale symphonic works, were greatly reduced in size compared to the orchestras that appeared in the concert hall. Acoustical recording techniques simply could not accommodate a hundred-piece orchestra. Nevertheless, by 1914, record companies were busily selling multirecord editions of the traditionally popular symphonic works of Beethoven, Brahms, Tchaikovsky and other composers.

It must be remembered that the listening experience

of our grandfathers and great-grandfathers some fifty years ago was not so sophisticated as is ours in the electronic age. They certainly knew how an orchestra should sound in a concert hall, yet they considered a recording of a Schubert symphony played by eight violins and two violas, without any regard for loud or soft passages, to be an audio miracle. Records were expected to sound unique and unrealistic, just as today we expect an electronic synthesizer to sound unique and unrealistic.

Nineteen fourteen ushered in a period of profound change in the recording industry. The broadening scope of the recorded repertoire was stimulating even greater record and equipment sales. Now a second depression struck the world, but record company executives scarcely felt the pinch; Victor's sales that year were better than ever. Most European nations were now plunged into the beginnings of World War I, while the United States began a futile effort to remain unentangled. The war gradually began to effect great economic change, even in the American record business, which went on to enjoy even greater prosperity and expansion.

A previous development in the American music publishing industry was also beginning to affect the economics of the record trade. A few years before, when residents of Tin Pan Alley in New York — songwriters, lyric writers and publishers — finally recognized the fact that records were big business, they also recognized that the major source of their income, the sale of sheet music, should be augmented by record royalties. Led by John Philip Sousa and the popular operetta composer Victor Herbert, a lobby was formed in Washington, and Congress was persuaded to enact a law that allowed composers and publishers a royalty of 2 cents per copy sold of recordings of their music properties. The law was passed in 1909, and, surprisingly, it has remained unchanged since.

Another sign of changing times was the death in 1915 of Edward D. Easton, one of the cofounders of the Columbia Phonograph Company.

A new wave of market competition also provided stimulus and change in the record business. Between 1914 and 1916, many of the basic recording patents controlled by either Victor or Columbia lapsed. This development encouraged a rash of newly formed equipment and record manufacturers to spring up. The public was suddenly introduced to several totally new record labels: Sonora, Aeolian, Vocalion and Brunswick. The Pathé brothers established a branch in New York, and the fast-growing Lindstrom Record Group of Germany founded an American subsidiary label, Okeh Records.

This swarm of new competitors did not ruffle the executives at either Victor or Columbia for the simple reason that the war seemed to have stimulated enough business for everybody. High-priced Victrolas, and even Edison Amberolas, were snapped up by a prosperous but entertainment-starved public.

On the other side of the Atlantic, England was also experiencing a record boom. An American named Louis Sterling had some years before joined the staff of the English branch of Columbia records. Like a number of other American record men, he adapted well to the English business climate, and quickly rose to the top job in the company.

Sterling was to make many important contributions to the record industry. Two of these developed in 1915. That year he signed a contract with Thomas Beecham, who was to become one of the greatest and most innovative conductors in the field of serious music.

During the early days of the war in England, London was brimming with troops. Sterling demonstrated his keen business sense again in 1915 when he noticed that one of the chief diversions for the soldiers, and indeed for native Londoners, was that of attending local musical revues. Crowds of soldiers and civilians lined up day and night to buy tickets. Why not, thought Sterling, record the songs from the revues as they were actually sung by members of the cast? The records would be ideal souvenirs for people who had attended the revues.

Sterling tested his theory with recordings of a show called *Business As Usual*. The idea was an immediate success. Sales of the recordings were brisk, as they were for two other revues recorded by Sterling shortly thereafter — Irving Berlin's *Watch Your Step*, and *Cheep*, starring Beatrice Lillie. These recordings marked the beginning of one of the great traditions of the record business — original cast show albums.

Meanwhile, the war continued to stimulate innovation in the United States. In 1917, Victor decided to gamble on a new form of music in 4/4 time called "Jass." It had originated in the South, gone on to sweep the Midwest, and had now taken hold in New York, where it could be heard nightly at Reisenweber's posh restaurant on Columbus Circle. The music was black in origin, but the players, The Original Jass Band of New Orleans, were white. Their first record was entitled "the Livery Stable Blues," and it was an immediate hit. "Jass" had opened up completely new prospects for the record business.

A pre–World War I Victrola advertisement illustrating the dance craze of the era

However, the popularity of this sensational new music could not compare with the dance craze that had possessed the country since 1913. In thousands of front parlors across the nation, Saturday night meant rolling away the carpet in front of the Victrola for a family dance session to the sounds of the turkey trot, the one-step, the hesitation waltz and the exotic tango. Victor hired the world famous dance team of Vernon and Irene Castle to supervise their dance record series. Sentiment was also commercially viable. "I Didn't Raise My Boy to Be a Soldier," "Poor Butterfly" and "There's a Long, Long Trail A'Winding" sold hundreds of thousands of records. By the time World War I ended, the major record companies were registering undreamed-of profits.

Inevitably, the bubble burst. A postwar recession hit

the country toward the latter part of 1920. Columbia found itself in dire circumstances because of a huge inventory of unsalable machines. Once the acknowledged leader in the industry, now the company managed to survive only by resorting to borrowing money and selling off subsidiary companies. Somehow, the position of the mighty Victor company continued unchallenged. Eldridge Johnson actually managed to increase sales during this period of financial crisis.

The postwar slump appeared to be over by the later part of 1921. A wave of record and machine buying followed in the wake of a new musical craze — the "Jazz Rag." Straitlaced citizens regarded the new music as the work of the devil. Jazz purists, on the other hand, spurned it as a white interpretation of what had originally been a Negro musical form. They preferred "race music" records by black musicians like King Oliver, Kid Ory and Louis Armstrong on small, or "independent," record labels. Nonetheless, the general public flocked to record shops to buy the latest releases of Jazz Rag band leaders Paul Whiteman, Ted Lewis, Fred Waring and Vincent Lopez.

Meanwhile, progress continued to be made in the field of serious music. Acoustical recording techniques were now so improved that symphony orchestras could be recorded without substituting woodwinds and brasses for stringed instruments. Nor was it any longer necessary to reduce the size of the orchestra to accommodate the limitations of the recording horn. Today, the symphonic recordings of the early twenties seem relatively dull and lifeless. But to the record fan of the era they represented the culmination of great technical progress, and they were a sheer delight to the ear.

8

The End of the Golden Age

I n 1923, the record industry reached the age of forty-six. It was now a comfortably prosperous business and it had developed some of the characteristics of successful middle-age: it was well-established, complacent, narrow-minded, self-satisfied and tending to be too fat for its own good. Certainly, record executives gave no indication that they were tough-thinking or imaginative enough to cope with the astounding impact of the newest home entertainment medium — radio. The first commercial radio broadcasts were heard on Pittsburgh's KDKA in 1919. Only three years later, radio stations were operating throughout the country, and sales of radio sets for the year totaled in the tens of millions.

At first there had seemed to be little for the recording industry to worry about. The early broadcasts were amateurish and plagued by static. The broadcast medium could not come close to matching the sophisticated productions offered by record companies. Even more reassuring was the fact that sales of popular record hits were apparently not affected. Radio would be hard put to match Paul Whiteman's recording of "Three O'Clock in the Morning," Moran and Mac's "Two Black Crows," the Okeh Laughing Record, Al Jolson's "Sonny Boy," Gene Auslin's "My Blue Heaven" or Vernon Dalhart's "Wreck of the Old '97." To the dedicated record fan, radio seemed no more than a passing fad.

Yet the new "squawk box" was serving notice that things would never be the same again. The first indication of change was the financial collapse of the Columbia Phonograph Company in 1923. Severely crippled by the postwar recession and the competition from radio, Columbia had managed to survive only by selling off its valuable subsidiaries. These desperate measures merely postponed the inevitable. Finally forced to file for bankruptcy, Columbia continued to operate under the direction of receivers, a court appointed panel assigned the responsibility of protecting the interests of the company's creditors.

The Victor Talking Machine Company preferred to ignore Columbia's misfortunes. But when radio set sales exploded from $60,000,000 in 1923 to $350,000,000 in 1924, Victor suffered a 20 percent drop in sales. The smaller manufacturers quickly accepted the reality of the situation. Sonora and Brunswick announced that they would begin to manufacture radio-phonograph combinations immediately. Victor still refused to budge. It was rumored at the time that company policy was so anti-radio that no Victor staff member dared to own a radio set.

In Victor's defense, it should be pointed out that radio program production in the mid-1920s was amateurish to say the least. But Victor executives failed to acknowledge two important facts that had not escaped the general public: the quality of the sound produced by radio's electrical circuitry, static and all, was by this time superior to the sound produced by the most expensive acoustical phonograph; and the programs offered by radio were, unlike records, totally free of charge.

By the end of 1924, the unofficial war between the radio and the phonograph for dominance in the home entertainment market was as good as finished. The combined sale of players and records had dropped to 50 percent of what it had been the previous year. Victor and Columbia were forced to drastically curtail their domestic recording programs. Both companies elected to rely mainly on the recording output of their European affiliates, who were as yet less affected by the impact of radio.

Once again the record business appeared to be in its death throes. But ironically it was research inspired by radio that led scientists to seek new applications for electrical circuitry that would inject new life into the industry again.

Since 1919, a team of Bell Laboratory engineers under the supervision of Joseph P. Maxfield had been secretly conducting experiments with electrical recording. Similar research was also under way in England at both His Master's Voice (formerly the Gramophone Company Ltd.) and at Louis Sterling's English Columbia Company. Although none of the research teams knew of the existence of the others, they shared a common goal: to utilize electrical energy to enhance acoustical power.

The three basic acoustical recording components — recording horn, diaphragm and cutting stylus — were replaced by a condenser microphone, a vacuum tube amplifier and an electromagnetically controlled cutting stylus.

The Bell system functioned in the following way. Mechanical energy in the form of sound waves was collected by the microphone's condenser. An electromagnetic coil, housed in the microphone, translated the sound waves into electrical impulses, which were relayed by wire to the amplifier, where they were greatly increased in magnitude. These stepped-up impulses were then conveyed by wire to the electromagnetically controlled cutting head. There they were reconverted into the mechanical energy required to drive the cutting stylus forming the record grooves.

An electric record player functioned somewhat similarly. A pickup unit consisting of the playback needle and an electromagnetic coil (sometimes a crystal was used) translated the groove-induced vibrations of the needle into electrical impulses. These were relayed by wire through the tone arm to the amplifier, where they were greatly strengthened and sent on to the speaker; there the speaker converted the electrical impulses into mechanical energy in the form of sound waves.

Since the energy generated by the electrical process was far greater than anything possible by the acoustical method, the electrically cut grooves were able to contain much higher levels of sound and a much wider dynamic range. It was now possible for the listener to hear on recordings both higher and lower frequencies of sound than ever before. Maxfield was certain that electricity would extend the limits of recorded sound to the extent that one would be able to listen to a record and hear *all* of the dynamic shadings and tone colors intended by the composer.

In 1924, Maxfield concluded that his team had developed the Bell system sufficiently to make it commercially viable. He believed that the major American record firms, Columbia and Victor, would leap at the chance to license the rights to use the new recording technique.

But Maxfield was wrong. Columbia, still staggering from repeated financial setbacks, was in a state of near atrophy, and the Bell system, with its wires, tubes and condensers, smacked far too much of that old devil radio to suit executives at Victor.

However, Maxfield's spectacular achievement was not to go unnoticed. The first man to fully realize the enormous importance of the system was English Columbia's Louis Sterling.

Sterling had already spent a fortune on electrical recording research. In December 1924, when he heard of Maxfield's new development, Sterling set sail for New York. When he arrived, he discovered that Bell, through its licensing and manufacturing affiliate, the Western Electric Company, intended to license the system only to American record firms. Under this arrangement, the American firms would be in a position to control sub-licensing rights abroad. Sterling also learned that Columbia had already been offered a license. Without hesitating, Sterling, with American financial help, bought a controlling interest in American Columbia for $2,500,000. His right to use the system in Europe was thus assured. Columbia signed a Bell license immediately after Sterling gained control of the company.

Now, after a singularly disastrous Christmas season in

1924, Victor had second thoughts. Eldridge Johnson signed a license with Western Electric a few weeks after Columbia.

Though Victor and Columbia began recording electrically early in 1925, both companies decided to keep their use of the process a secret. They feared that publicizing the revolutionary new process would render obsolescent existing stocks of acoustical records. Victor quietly released several electrical "pop" recordings in May 1925, without mentioning the fact that they had been recorded in the new medium. Among the titles was "Let It Rain; Let It Pour," by Meyer Davis and his orchestra. Two months later, Victor released the first electrical symphonic recording, Leopold Stokowski and the Philadelphia Orchestra's performance of Saint-Saens's "Danse Macabre." The public, still unaware of what was going on, did not react. However, a sensational new record on Columbia quickly changed matters.

With much fanfare, Columbia released a "live" performance of "Adeste Fidelis" by a combined group of college glee clubs recorded on the stage of the old Metropolitan Opera House in New York. The buildup given the record was worthwhile, for in a short time it became an international best seller. Unlike an acoustical recording, its sound had depth, brightness and realism. Astute record buyers now knew beyond a doubt that something startlingly new had happened.

From an outsider's point of view, the transition in the industry from acoustical to electrical recordings appeared to be gradual. However, this was certainly not so within the confines of the recording studio. Here the change was drastic and abrupt. Suddenly, an atmosphere of spacious-

An early electrical recording session

ness prevailed. The microphone was capable of capturing the sound of even the softest pianissimo on the violin, so it was no longer necessary to crowd studio musicians together in front of the horn. The stroh-violin became as extinct as the dodo. It was as though the window of a hot, stuffy room were opened for the first time.

Yet, in spite of the obvious advantages of electrical recording techniques, there were more than a few record fans who lamented the passing of the acoustical era. And it must be admitted that the acoustical record had demanded a kind of honesty of its vocal performers. To be effective, a singer or an actor had to have been able to project his or her voice. (This undoubtedly had been a common capability among the stage performers of the

85

day, as there were no microphones in theaters or opera houses, either.) With electrical recording, this ability was no longer necessary.

The electrical microphone was soon to alter performing styles in several areas of entertainment. Read and Welch, in their monumental history of recordings, *From Tin Foil to Stereo*, sum up the sudden change rather succinctly:

> The insinuating *sotto voce*, over-amplified sounds made by "Whispering Jack Smith and Little Jack Little," represented the more obvious misuses of the microphone technics eventually to be foisted on the public. Rudy Vallee was to popularize the term "Crooner" and open the doors of recording studios to a flood of trick stylists from radio. The trend became epidemic. Soon stage appearances had to be bolstered with public address systems, for without amplification the crooning Mills Brothers and Miss Poop-poop-a-do could not have been heard beyond the third row.

Bolstered or not, the sounds produced by electrical circuitry were immediately popular with most of the public. The Bell system excited a rash of large-scale recordings both in Europe and the United States.

Meanwhile, by 1925, optimistic record men were convinced that radio and records could live and prosper side by side. Certainly developments in 1926 seemed to bear out this theory. Eldridge Johnson finally conceded that radio would last. On his approval, Victor began to manufacture radio-phonograph consoles comprised of Radiolas purchased from the Radio Corporation of America and

Electrolas, Victor's first electric record player. It proved to be a happy wedding. Sales of Victor Talking Machine products soared that year. Even the troubled Columbia Phonograph Company seemed to be on the road to recovery.

The rapid comeback of the record industry did not go unnoticed in other business quarters. A group of Wall Street bankers approached Eldridge Johnson with a proposal to purchase the Victor Talking Machine Company. For years, Johnson had rejected offers to sell his controlling interest in the firm. But now, to everyone's amazement, Johnson agreed to accept the Wall Street offer, and other Victor shareholders complied. Reportedly, Johnson received $28,000,000 for his personal share in the business. The reasons for his decision to sell remain clouded. Some historians believe that he decided to retire for reasons of health — although he lived on until 1945. However, it is possible that he accurately foresaw the approach of a disastrous period for the industry, and decided to get out while the getting, as they say, was good. In any event, Johnson's departure from Victor after so many years appeared to have little effect on the company. Business continued to flourish without him.

By now Victor had clearly demonstrated a continuing ability to make respectable profits, as well as operate highly efficient manufacturing and distribution facilities. This was enough to convince those at the helm of the new industrial giant, the Radio Corporation of America, that the Victor Talking Machine Company would be an ideal addition to their fast-growing empire. Following nine months of negotiations, the two companies merged, with RCA in command.

It appeared that an exciting new era in the history of recorded sound was in the offing as the two industrial leaders began to pool their considerable resources. But the road ahead seemed even more golden when record makers discovered a fresh, new source of hit song material. Their treasure trove was the Hollywood musical film.

The first commercial film to offer sound synchronized with pictures was the legendary *Jazz Singer*, starring Al Jolson. As soon as Warner Brothers released the film in 1927, it was an absolute sensation. At the time Jolson was an established recording star for Brunswick Records. To help promote the film, he recorded several of the songs he had sung in the picture at Brunswick's studios. Virtually every one became a hit, including a song written specifically for the film, "Mother of Mine, I Love You." The following year, Fanny Brice recorded several songs from the sound track of her first motion picture, *My Man*, for RCA Victor, with almost the same spectacular results obtained by Jolson. But the most fertile source of hit record material turned out to be Metro-Goldwyn-Mayer's history-making musical *The Broadway Melody*, starring Bessie Love, Anita Page and Charles King. Hundreds of thousands of movie fans jammed motion picture theaters newly wired for sound to hear and see the principals perform "You Were Meant for Me," "The Wedding Song of the Painted Doll" and other tunes. The record companies rushed to their studios to turn out dance and vocal versions of the song titles featured in the film.

Some modern record historians have been puzzled by the fact that at the time not one record company made an attempt to obtain rights to the original sound track, preferring to rerecord the songs. This course of action may have been prompted by technical difficulties or professional jealousy — or simply because no one had thought of it.

In any case, the phenomenal success of the early Hollywood musicals encouraged a flood of new motion pictures brimming with song. Record companies reacted to the stimulus quickly. Recording activity revolved around Hollywood personalities, and had risen to a fever pitch by 1929. That year, Brunswick released several records of Al Jolson singing songs from his latest film, *Say It With Music*.

Columbia's releases in 1929 also reflected a strong Hollywood orientation. There was Ethel Waters's record of "Am I Blue" from *On With the Show*; and a collection of Cliff "Ukelele" Ike Edwards's (who later became the voice of Jiminy Cricket in Walt Disney's *Pinocchio*) recordings of songs from his two current film successes, *So This Is College* and *The Hollywood Revue of 1929*. Another Columbia record release of note — one that was to become a classic — was band leader Ted Lewis's recording of the title song from his film *Is Everybody Happy?* A point of historical interest is the fact that Columbia's releases that year also included records by Ken Maynard, performing songs from a film called *The Wagon Master*. They were the first records ever made by a Hollywood cowboy star.

RCA Victor was also very much in evidence on the Hollywood scene of the late twenties. Victor executives signed recording contracts with Jeanette MacDonald and Maurice Chevalier, the young singing stars of a hit musical film, *The Love Parade*. Shortly thereafter, several equally important film entertainers were added to the company's artist roster: Helen Morgan, who had cata-pulted to stardom in a film entitled *Applause*; Sophie Tucker, the perennial record favorite who was then being featured in a picture called *Honky Tonk*; Bebe Daniels, the star of *Rio Rita*; and Rudy Vallee, the famous crooner.

9

The Crash—and the Long Road Back

As 1929 drew to a close, the future of the record business appeared more promising than ever. Most American businesses were booming. The country appeared to be in a state of limitless prosperity. There were stories of elevator operators, shoe-shine boys and bellhops who had accumulated fortunes in a constantly rising stock market. Only a handful of economic experts warned that excessive credit buying had driven the prices of stocks and bonds far beyond their actual worth.

The moment of truth came in October 1929. The stock market collapsed and the economy of the United States, and indeed of most of the rest of the world, began a period of severe decline. The golden promise of the record business suddenly disappeared as if it had been a mirage. Now began the darkest chapter in the history of recorded sound.

The first notable casualty of the depression was the Thomas A. Edison Company. In 1930, all commercial phonograph and record manufacturing activities in West Orange, New Jersey, ceased. But the depression merely dealt the final blow to an already dying company. The eighty-two-year-old inventor had resisted electrical recordings as stubbornly as he had resisted radio and the flat disc record. In 1927 he had attempted to counter these innovations with an announcement that he had developed a record capable of containing twenty minutes of music on each side. Though he promised this long-playing record would be released shortly, it was an as yet unrealized dream. Edison did, in fact, design a record with three times the usual number of grooves per side. But he insisted that it revolve at 80 revolutions per minute, so as not to make obsolete the thousands of Edison phonographs that were designed for that speed already in circulation. Since playback styluses simply could not track the extremely narrow, constricted grooves, the venture ended in failure. After 1930, the Thomas A. Edison Company's activities were confined to the manufacture and development of office dictation machines. It was the one goal his "baby" had realized that he would never surrender during his remaining years.

The depression took its toll of a number of other record companies, among them Okeh Records. The activities of those companies that continued to operate during the depression were severely hampered. Victor appeared to lose much of its individuality in RCA's shadow. Columbia was once again struggling to stay alive, and Brunswick was looking for a buyer. Fortunately, an angel appeared in the form of the Warner Brothers film company, an organization still flushed with the success of its sound pictures. Warner Brothers executives were convinced that the motion picture and record industries were compatible, since records were obviously an ideal promotional vehicle for film stars. They bought Brunswick in 1930. The film company's assessment of the potential of records was accurate; however, it was decidedly premature.

Although the effects of the depression were less severe in Europe, English Columbia and His Master's Voice decided that merger and consolidation were the keys to survival. Both companies had already absorbed a number of smaller competitors, including English Columbia's purchase of the Pathé Brothers in 1925. The two giant companies married in 1931, and their offspring, Electrical and Musical Industries (E.M.I.) became the world's largest international record cartel. Its chief executive was the irrepressible American Louis Sterling, who was now a British subject and who would one day be awarded a knighthood. Sterling's only remaining competition in continental Europe was the German record combine, Deutsche Grammophon Gesellschaft–Polydor, which, ironically, had once been a member of the Gramophone Company Ltd. family. By the same token, E.M.I.'s only competition in the British Isles was a new record company founded in London in 1929 — Decca, which first specialized in manufacturing low-priced records.

In the United States, desperate record executives began planning ways to fend off disaster. Late in 1931, RCA Victor, taking a cue from Edison, announced an important new concept — a long-playing record. Lowering the rate of speed from the recently accepted industry standard of 78 revolutions per minute to 33⅓ in effect doubled the playing time of the new record. It may be recalled that Edison's refusal to reduce the speed of his earlier long-playing record had led to its downfall.

Despite considerable fanfare, the RCA Victor attempt also proved a fiasco. One serious drawback to the new disc was that there simply were not enough machines in circulation capable of adapting to the new speed. A few phonograph models were equipped with a special device that could shift the machine's speed from 78 to 33⅓, but there were not enough of these models around to give the revolutionary disc a fair trial. Nor did RCA Victor attempt to manufacture a 33⅓ player. But the main flaw in the new LP's ill-starred campaign was its interaction with the extremely heavy tone arm of the thirties. The few customers who sampled the LPs discovered that the plastic pressings wore out after only a few plays. RCA Victor wisely withdrew the records from its catalogue the following year.

Even if Victor had launched the long-playing record successfully, there is no reason to suspect that the downward spiral of the record business could have been halted. By 1932, the economic state of the country was so bad that hundreds of banks were forced to close. Previously employed professional men were reduced to selling apples on street corners in every city of the United States. The retail market, except for those stores dealing in essential products, was decimated. In those hard times, records were hardly considered essential fare to a family in need of food and clothing.

But the sad plight of the record trade appeared to be the result of more than just depressed economic conditions. The public seemed to have grown tired of records. They were considered outdated and no longer fashionable. When comparing radio to records, people often referred to radio as "live" entertainment and to records disparagingly as "canned" music. High-level RCA executives were convinced that radio had just about eliminated the record from the home entertainment scene. Why, they asked, would anyone buy the latest dance record when the same music could be heard for free on the air? This viewpoint seemed to be borne out as phonographs gradually disappeared from living rooms and front parlors and, along with stacks of records, were stored away in the dusty recesses of attics and cellars.

E.M.I.'s reaction to the seemingly hopeless situation was to sell the entire American Columbia facility to Majestic Radio. The fall of the once-autonomous Columbia label seemed a sign that the end of the record was at hand. But the record business was to prove a lot tougher and more durable than the proponents of radio had ever imagined.

In the past, the recording industry had at each crisis escaped extinction by the discovery of an improvement in or a new use for recorded sound. Now, at its sorriest moment in history, it was to be rescued by faith. Two men emerged to lead the American record industry out of the doldrums. They shared two things: they both had acquired their experience in the record business working for Brunswick, and they each had an unquenchable enthusiasm for the future of recording. Their names were Edward Wallerstein and Jack Kapp.

By 1930 Wallerstein, whose contributions to the industry were to prove the more far-reaching of the two men's, had worked his way up from the lower ranks at Brunswick to the post of sales manager. In 1932, at a time when the record business was at its lowest ebb, he left Brunswick to take over the record operation at RCA Victor. One of his first decisions was to discontinue the company's abortive attempt to promote long-playing records. Wallerstein sincerely believed that the long-playing record would one day be feasible — a conviction that was to have a profound influence on the record business in the future. But for the present, he lived by the motto that records ought to provide "the music you want to hear, *when* you want to hear it." He seemed to know instinctively that the public would soon grow tired of waiting hours, or even days, to hear the hit tunes they loved broadcast on radio stations. He also knew that there was a sizable potential market of classical music record collectors — a market that had not been tapped in years.

Wallerstein's ideas were soon put into action. Once again, a small but steady flow of new record releases began reaching record dealers' shelves. For the first time since the black days of the early 1930s, RCA Victor began to publish catalogues that described the contents of forthcoming releases and listed the numbers and titles of those backlist records that were still available. Wallerstein had to fight the radio-oriented establishment at RCA to reinstate this simple, but vitally important, service.

But his biggest handicap was simply that there were not enough working record players in circulation. New machines would be particularly difficult to sell during this period of diminished wages and high unemployment. Economic conditions were better, but America was still fighting its way out of the depression.

The solution, thought Wallerstein, was to exploit the existence of 20,000,000 radio sets currently in use in American homes. They could provide the speakers and amplifiers for inexpensive turntables. The result was the Duo, Jr., a record player without tubes or speaker that was designed to be jacked into radio sets. RCA Victor offered the little players at a retail price of $16.50 each, but more often record dealers sold them at cost to stimulate customers to buy more records. It was an early example of the American business philosophy of giving away the razor to sell the blades. The Duo, Jr., converted thousands of people to the hobby of record collecting, and contributed importantly to the recovery of the record business.

Jack Kapp, creative director at Brunswick, was another who invested his faith in the record industry during these dark days, though not without considerable assistance from E. R. Lewis, the head of the London-based Decca Records Company.

In 1934, Lewis learned that Majestic Radio was interested in selling Columbia Records. Through American business intermediaries, he negotiated a purchase price of $75,000. Upon his ship's arrival in New York only one week later, on July 6, 1934, Lewis was informed much to his chagrin that while he was at sea, Majestic had sold Columbia to the American Record Company for only $70,500.

Three years earlier, Warner Brothers had licensed to the American Record Company the right to use the Brunswick trademark and to sell Brunswick records. Lewis, determined that his trip to New York should not be wasted, bought from Warner's the rights to the Brunswick trademark and that portion of the Brunswick record catalogue that was still owned by Warner's. This catalogue provided Lewis with a base of operations for the American branch of Decca which he founded in New

York that August. He then prevailed upon Jack Kapp, the brilliant creative director of Brunswick, to manage the new company.

The founding of an American branch of Decca did a great deal to raise the morale of the handful of record store owners who still managed to eke out an existence during the depression. They sensed that the infusion of new blood into the ailing business meant that better days were in the offing, even though Lewis's stated policy would bring lower profit margins. Based on his experience in England, Lewis was convinced that records did not have to be expensive to be good. Now Decca popular music records would be sold for thirty-five cents each, a considerable reduction from the seventy-five-cent price tag attached to most other popular record labels.

Jack Kapp must have been an extremely persuasive man. It was not long before a number of the most popular recording stars, some of whom had met Kapp earlier at Brunswick, broke off their relationships with other record companies to sign contracts with Decca. The artist roster of the new company was impressive. It included Bing Crosby, the Dorsey brothers, Guy Lombardo, the Mills Brothers, Fletcher Henderson, and Arthur Tracey, the famous "Street Singer."

The combination of top stars and bargain prices created new distribution outlets for the young company. The five and dime store became a prime factor in the business: by 1936, tubby-sounding, bass-heavy record players could be heard throughout the land, blaring forth melodies over the whir of malted milk mixers and the clang of cash registers. Records were once again available to the masses.

10

The Renaissance

PERHAPS THE GREATEST stimulus to the revival of records in the thirties was the reintroduction of coin-operated record players. The repeal of Prohibition in 1933 triggered the opening of thousands of bars and cocktail lounges. Salesmen visited these new establishments, offering in each to install a juke box,* a coin machine with the capability of selecting and playing a variety of record titles automatically. The advantage of these machines was twofold: they provided an establishment's patrons with low-cost entertainment, and they furnished the owner with an additional source of income. It was, of course, an ingenious idea, and virtually every bar owner in the country capitulated. Juke boxes quickly spread to other business locations catering to the public: diners, drugstores, restaurants and the like.

* It is believed that the word "juke" is derived from the African word "jook," which means disorderly.

Before long, the juke box evolved into a major source of entertainment away from home. In those hard times, a record fan might not have been able to afford the seventy-five cents or even the thirty-five cents necessary to buy a record, but he could usually spare a nickel to hear his favorite recording while he sipped a glass of beer or munched a hamburger. In these years the fan's favorite record might have been Bing Crosby's "Love in Bloom" from the crooner's latest hit motion picture, *She Loves Me Not*; or he might have preferred Fred Astaire's "I'm Putting All My Eggs in One Basket" or "Let's Call the Whole Thing Off," both from Astaire's immensely popular films costarring Ginger Rogers. If our record fan were sharp-eared, he would have detected that the recorded versions of these songs were quite different from the versions heard in the films. Choruses and grand orchestral arrangements were absent on records for the simple reason that the record companies could not afford them.

The proliferation of the juke box had some effect on the design of playback equipment in general. The quality of recorded sound did not change much: the machines were still bass-heavy and generally limited in dynamic range, although they were rugged and built to last. But equipment manufacturers were now forced to design a playback needle that could be used for hundreds of playings without having to be changed. Besides meeting a need in the juke box business, this advance in needle manufacture also proved a boon to the home entertainment market.

The juke box was of immense importance to the industry in other ways, as well. It provided a ready market for record manufacturers and it functioned as a vital promotional vehicle. People began to buy the records they had heard at the local bar or drugstore. *Billboard* and *Variety*, two of the entertainment trade's most important journals, began tabulating juke box operator sales returns. This enabled record store owners to anticipate hit records. Top recording stars began to follow the returns to discover which new song titles the public preferred. Producers of radio programs, particularly those involved in the production of musical shows, now followed the juke box charts in order to determine more accurately "coming hits" or "sleepers."

The American record business appeared to be on the upswing, despite the fact that in 1936 more records were imported from England than were actually manufactured in the entire United States. At any rate, RCA Victor was sufficiently encouraged to publish a sales report for the first time in years. With guarded optimism, the company announced that it had sold 1,200,000 records in December 1936, about 25 percent of which were classical. The rise in the sale of serious music recordings was attributable to the return to the Victor recording studio of the great conductor Arturo Toscanini. The "Maestro's" multiple-record album of Beethoven's Symphony No. 7, which also included orchestral works by Wagner, Rossini and Brahms, sold more than two thousand copies in New York City alone. But this could still not compare to Victor's sales of Benny Goodman's current hit single, "One O'Clock Jump." Even more dramatic were sales of Louis Prima's "The Music Goes Round and Round," the first record to break the 100,000 sales barrier since Al Jolson's "Sonny Boy" back in the golden twenties.

Since the earliest days, record makers had been content

to take on hits created in other entertainment media, whether the Hollywood film, radio, the Broadway stage, vaudeville, the medicine show or the bandstand. Tin Pan Alley song pluggers had naturally concentrated their promotional efforts in these other media. In fact, in the mid-thirties, it was considered a greater promotional coup to have saleswomen of five-and-dime sheet music demonstrate a new song title at the piano (a fairly common chain store fixture in the thirties) than it was to convince a record producer to record the song with a top artist. Now, with the revival of the record business, the picture steadily changed; the promotion staffs of music publishers began to shift their attention to records. As indicated before, by becoming an important promotional vehicle, the juke box greatly enhanced the status of records. From the late 1930s until the outbreak of World War II, the growth of the record business paralleled the enormous expansion of the juke box industry. There were 255,000 machines in operation in 1939; they utilized 13,000,000 records and stimulated the home consumption of millions of additional discs. And Tin Pan Alley had found another reason to pay closer attention to records: a practice of programming music was growing among radio stations — over the objections of record company executives, it might be added.

Meanwhile, Hollywood continued to provide invaluable source material for the recording market. It was Jack Kapp at Decca, always clever and enterprising, who capitalized on a new way of presenting Hollywood musical fare. In 1938, RCA Victor released three records from the original sound track of Walt Disney's *Snow White and the Seven Dwarfs*. Kapp, aware that under federal law a

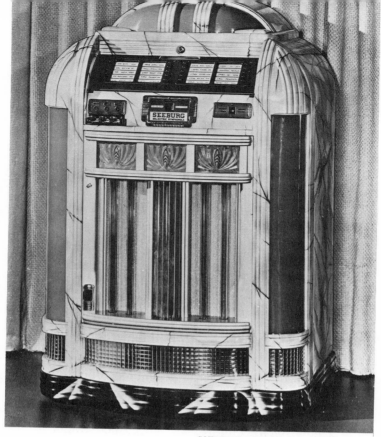

A Seeburg juke box, circa 1940

musical copyright could not be denied to a record company once the first recorded version had been released, quickly produced his own versions of the songs from *Snow White* on Decca's label. They proved almost as successful as the originals. Kapp followed the same pattern with Disney's next feature-length cartoon, *Pinocchio*. However, Kapp resorted to the practice of producing studio versions of sound tracks only when he failed to acquire the rights to the originals for Decca. A case in point is the famous film *The Wizard of Oz*, starring Judy Garland. The original sound track was acquired by Kapp and is still available on Decca records.

Jack Kapp's shrewd sense of commercial repertoire and his excellent business judgment had brought Decca to the point where it was seriously challenging RCA Victor for leadership in the industry. But a far more serious threat to Victor's supremacy lay within its own organization. Edward Wallerstein, who along with Jack Kapp had done so much to revive the record business in the deep depression years, had become dissatisfied with his lot at RCA Victor, and was casting about for other things to occupy his time. He became intrigued with the idea of rebuilding the once mighty Columbia Phonograph Company, currently in the hands of the American Record Company.

The Columbia label, although it ranked third in total sales, lagged far behind its two major competitors, RCA Victor and Decca. However, Wallerstein felt that Columbia could provide him with the facilities he needed to forge a new record empire: an established trademark; a pressing plant in Bridgeport, Connecticut; and the rights to sell English Columbia's recordings in the United States. To realize his plans, Wallerstein needed financial backing, and he acquired it through William S. Paley, the president of the rapidly growing Columbia Broadcasting System. Wallerstein and Paley agreed in principle, but they still had to pass the hurdle posed by the radio network's board of directors. A number of the board members thought that the price for Columbia, over $700,000, was excessive, considering that the same property had been sold only four years previously for a tenth of that amount. Then, too, Columbia was at the time a moribund company offering little competition to the other labels. Nevertheless, Paley and Wallerstein prevailed upon the board, and in December 1938, the purchase was made; one which CBS was never to question again or regret.

Wallerstein immediately assumed command of the rejuvenated company, and moved swiftly to bolster its position in all categories of recorded entertainment. He persuaded some of the top names in "swing" and "big band" music to join the label; among them were Benny Goodman, Duke Ellington and Count Basie. Contrary to Decca's precedent, the new Columbia artists were to be featured on a special red-label series selling for fifty cents, as opposed to the thirty-five cents now standardly charged by many popular-record companies. But customers got their money's worth. The red-label records, manufactured with a new laminating process, were far superior in sound and durability to any other popular record on the market. These were highly attractive features to the juke box operator, and to the thousands of people who owned record players with automatic changers. Both the juke box and the record changer of 1939 wreaked severe punishment on a shellac record.

Wallerstein's timing was superb. The record business was definitely on the upsurge in 1939. The big band era was in full swing, and the companies vied with each other to supply the growing market with the best in popular music. According to the July twentieth edition of *Billboard*, the best-selling record title of the day was Tommy Dorsey's "I'll Never Smile Again." The incomparable Glenn Miller, perhaps the greatest band leader of his time, was represented on the same top ten listing by three records, "Imagination," "Fools Rush In," and "Pennsylvania 6-5000." Only one vocal recording managed to hit that chart, and naturally, it was Bing Crosby, singing "Sierra Sue."

When Wallerstein became convinced that Columbia had a firm footing in the growing popular music business, he began formulating plans to break RCA Victor's hold on the classical record market. The three major American symphonic orchestras were already under contract to Victor: the Philadelphia Orchestra, the New York Philharmonic and the Boston Symphony Orchestra. Wallerstein had to be content to record the Cleveland Orchestra and the Chicago Symphony Orchestra. Serious record fans were unimpressed when, in March of 1940, these new recordings appeared in stores at the now standard classical record price of two dollars a record. RCA Victor's armor hadn't even been dented.

But the release of the new records at the old price was only the first step in Wallerstein's carefully calculated plan. He knew that classical record buyers were extremely price-conscious. He was also aware that RCA Victor was such a big factor in the classical record business that it had lost most of its flexibility. He bided his time. Then in August of 1940, he struck swiftly and accurately. A full-page ad in *Life* magazine announced that the price of all Columbia classical records had been halved. At the same time, Wallerstein directed his sales department to inform the record stores that stocked Columbia's classical product that the company would compensate them for the drop in value of their inventories. After all, he had very little to lose; as yet, few Columbia classical records were available in retail stores.

The reaction of the public to the *Life* ad was immediate and overwhelming. Thousands of serious music fans flocked to record stores to take Columbia up on its offer. After a considerable length of time, RCA Victor reluctantly reduced the unit price of its own Red Seal records to one dollar. However, the larger company made no mention of compensating dealers for the depreciation in the value of their inventories. As Wallerstein had calculated, there were far too many RCA Victor records in record stores to permit his rival to make such an offer.

Wallerstein's daring achieved two results: thousands of record collectors became conditioned to look to Columbia for serious music recordings; and the firm won the loyalty and enthusiastic support of most of the country's leading retailers. The success of the campaign became evident toward the end of 1941. Columbia reported that its classical record sales volume had increased elevenfold. Suddenly, the RCA Victor Red Seal enterprise was faced with real competition for the first time since the turn of the century.

The record industry was now on a solid footing; the three major companies were prospering and the future appeared excellent. Veteran record executives reasoned that the likely involvement of the United States in World War II would further stimulate business, just as it had been stimulated during World War I.

When the United States did, as predicted, enter the new world conflict, an entertainment-starved populace eager to spend money on records materialized once again. Ironically, the industry was not able to reap the benefits. Five months after the Japanese attack on Pearl Harbor on December 7, 1941, the federal government declared shellac a material vital to national defense. All ware-

A visit to the Columbia Records pressing plant in Bridge-
port, Connecticut, 1940. The press shown here is turning
out 78 rpm shellac records

houses in which the record pressing materials were stored
were locked and sealed by government agents. All production of radios, phonographs and juke boxes was also
halted. The record business would simply have to make
do with what it had.

Nevertheless, in the face of severe material shortages,
Glenn Wallichs decided to launch Capitol Records in
1942. The Capitol staff took a novel approach to the pro-

motion of their first record releases. They decided to take advantage of a new breed in the entertainment world, the disc jockey. Copies of the initial Capitol releases were sent to approximately fifty of the most influential deejays in the country.

Most of Capitol's competitors had made it a point to avoid the radio medium. In fact, most commercial record labels of the thirties carried a legend strictly prohibiting broadcast. Fred Waring, the famous orchestra and choral director, was in the process of suing the radio industry for playing his discs without permission or payment. Decca Records on a number of occasions had threatened to sue broadcasters for spinning the label's pop discs. The American Federation of Musicians, which had the most to lose if discs were to replace radio station musicians, preferred to ignore the problem. The union's leadership felt that they still exercised enough power over radio stations to control the situation.

But the trend to disc jockeys was inevitable. The great radio network variety shows of the era, featuring stars like Jack Benny, Eddie Cantor, Kate Smith, Fred Allen, Rudy Vallee, Ed Wynn, and Edgar Bergen and Charlie McCarthy were all extremely expensive to produce and were broadcast only during prime evening listening hours. Daytime radio fare consisted for the most part of dreary soap operas and organ music. Now, quality recordings, whether popular or classical, provided radio stations with more entertaining and more economical program material. Stations began to use more recorded material rather than less, despite the legal risks.

Then James Petrillo, the formidable leader of the 140,000-member American Federation of Musicians, decided to take matters into his own hands. Recalling the days before juke boxes, when thousands of restaurants and dance halls had employed musicians and most radio stations were staffed with live musicians, he declared a state of war against "canned" music.

Petrillo had no quarrel with the use of records for home entertainment; but he demanded that record companies prevent records from being played on juke boxes and radio stations. If they didn't, he would have his members vote to strike.

The record companies simply could not comply. They could not control radio station managements, nor were they in a position to surrender the lucrative record sales derived from the juke box industry. But Petrillo was not bluffing. When no action was taken, he called for a musicians' strike against the record companies on July 31, 1942.

The record companies were now reduced to existing on reissues and material culled from "iceboxes," record company jargon for recorded but unreleased material. However, since record companies traditionally plan releases months ahead of schedule, the number of unreleased recordings on hand was considerable. Thus, the record companies decided they were in a position to wait Petrillo out. An interesting footnote to the story is that, among other things, Petrillo ruled that the harmonica was not, in the union's eyes, a musical instrument. This decision spurred a rash of new recordings by harmonica soloists and groups.

On all other counts, Petrillo proved to be an intractable and resourceful foe. As time passed, the pressure on record executives steadily mounted as new songs began to be introduced to the public in rival media — the Broadway musical, the Hollywood film, and radio. Thirteen months after the moratorium, Decca began to feel the pinch. The war had completely severed relations between the American and the British branches of the company. American Decca was now an independent entity and was very much in need of popular hits to survive, unlike its competition at RCA Victor and Columbia. Finally, Decca was forced to capitulate to Petrillo, agreeing to pay the AFM a royalty on the sale of all records employing its members. The royalties were to be paid into a fund to be used to create employment for musicians in live concerts.

No sooner had the ink dried on the agreement than Decca recorded the original Broadway cast version of the Rodgers and Hammerstein hit musical *Oklahoma!* The sale of the album was predictably phenomenal. An entertainment-starved public avidly snapped up 1,000,000 copies of the album, and Decca was back again on the road to prosperity.

Despite Decca's defection, Columbia and Victor continued to resist Petrillo for another fourteen months, but without a united front the battle seemed hopeless. Finally, in the fall of 1944, Edward Wallerstein, Columbia's president, admitted that only two courses were open to him: settle with the union, or go out of business. Columbia came to terms — the same agreed to by Decca — and shortly thereafter RCA Victor followed suit.

Once peace was made, the record boom returned in greater strength than ever before. The end of the war in 1945 did nothing to stop the constantly rising spiral of record sales. The following year, shellac was once again being imported into the United States from India — this time in huge quantities.

Meanwhile, the heyday of the big band era was coming

Billie Holliday

to an end. The war and its demands on manpower had decimated the ranks of many bands. Tommy Dorsey, Artie Shaw, Harry James, Bob Crosby and the other great band leaders were gradually being replaced by the featured soloists or singing groups who had once graced their bandstands. Martha Tilton, Peggy Lee and Helen Ward rose to stardom after roles as "featured" vocalists with the "King of Swing," Benny Goodman. Frank Sinatra decided to strike out on his own in 1943, after serving apprenticeships with both the Tommy Dorsey and the Harry James bands. Dick Haymes was another crooner to utilize the Harry James organization as a ladder to fame. His hit records of "You'll Never Know" and "Little White Lies" soon catapulted him into starring roles in films. A singer named Perry Como followed in Sinatra's footsteps. Doris Day began as a featured singer with Les Brown's Orchestra, and Dinah Shore first sang with Xavier Cugat and his band. But the master hit-maker of the era was Tommy Dorsey, who now featured himself as a trombonist. Teaming up with Roy Eberle and Helen O'Connell, he created a skein of hit records, including "Green Eyes," "Amapola," "Tangerine," "Maria Elena" and "Yours." Numerous other vocal stars rose to fame during this period, among them: Pearl Bailey, Lena Horne, Ella Fitzgerald, Ginny Simms, Betty Hutton, Billie Holliday, Kay Starr, Harry Babbitt, Al Hibbler, and Skip Nelson — and the most popular of them all, Bing Crosby, then forty-two years old. He had fondly been dubbed "der Bingle" by his admirers.

11

The Revolution Begins

NINETEEN FORTY-SEVEN marked the seventieth birthday of the record industry. To the record man, the future appeared bright. Moreover, there seemed to be little need for innovation in the field. Looking back over the previous fifty years, an observer could see that, with the exception of the introduction of electrical recordings in 1925, there had been no significant changes in the business. In 1947, a twelve-inch record spinning at 78 revolutions per minute was capable of a maximum playing time per side of approximately four and a half minutes. A twelve-inch disc record, circa 1903, had nearly the same capacity. Nor were there many innovations on the creative side of making records. Producers were reluctant to use the medium to introduce new artists or songs. They still preferred to "borrow" their successes from other worlds of entertainment.

Nevertheless, important changes were already taking place, and the record trade was about to undergo a revolution that would culminate in the reestablishment of recorded sound as one of the most important forms of mass entertainment.

One of the key factors in the revolution dated from the development by German scientists of a workable tape recorder. American engineers, following in the wake of the Allied invasion of Germany in 1944, discovered that a number of German radio stations were equipped with Magnetophone tape recorders. The engineers were not particularly surprised by the existence of the machines, since the theory of electromagnetic tape recording had been known for decades. What amazed them was the rapidity with which the Germans had converted theory into practical application.

By recording industry standards today, the Magnetophone recorder was a cumbersome contraption. It utilized fourteen-inch reels of iron-oxide-coated plastic tape, and it operated at a high rate of speed — 30 inches per second. But the Magnetophone was nonetheless an efficient, commercially viable piece of electronic equipment. Its sound capabilities equalled those of the best electrically produced records of the era.

The Magnetophone, and all subsequent tape recorders for that matter, operated as follows. A microphone collected sound waves, amplified them, and applied them to a recording head. The head consisted of a coil of wire wound around a ring made of readily magnetized metallic material. The ring was broken by a tiny gap measuring no more than 1/1000 of an inch. When the amplified electrical impulses were applied to the coil, the pulsating electrical current flowing through it created a fluctuating magnetic field across the gap. A loud sound created an intense electromagnetic impulse, and so on. The actual recording medium, the iron-oxide-coated plastic tape, passed through the varying magnetic field at a constant speed. Each of the millions of minute oxide particles on the surface of tape was magnetized to the extent of the intensity of the field at the split second it passed under the recording head.

To re-create the sound magnetized on the tape, the process was simply reversed. The recorded tape was passed under the reproducing, or playback, head at the same rate of speed that had been maintained during the recording phase. The magnetic field surrounding the tape created a magnetic flux in the core of the metallic ring of the playback head. This varying flux in turn induced electromagnetic impulses in the coil of wire wound around the ring. These impulses were then amplified to the extent that they were of sufficient strength to drive a speaker, and thus the sounds originally recorded were re-created.

The pioneer of magnetic recording had been a Danish scientist named Valdemar Poulsen, who built a primitive wire recorder called the Telegraphone in 1889. The machine utilized demagnetized steel wire rather than tape, since tape was to require years of further development before it was perfected. Although Poulsen's machine did most assuredly work, it was condemned to obscurity. It predated by many years the condenser microphone and the vacuum tube amplifier, both vital components of magnetic recording. Unfortunately, the quality of the sound produced by the Telegraphone was never better than that of the 1900 model of the telephone. For that reason the whole concept of magnetic recording was shelved for decades.

It was the success of radio and electrical recordings that was to renew interest in magnetic recording techniques, particularly in Germany. There is no doubt that most of the credit for the modern tape recorder is due to pre–World War II German science. Yet it was American expertise that was to produce the refinements necessary to make the tape recorder a practical instrument in the recording studio and the home.

Over a period of three years, a team of Minnesota Mining and Manufacturing Company engineers worked tirelessly on the improvement of the quality of magnetic tape. They ultimately developed a tape with characteristics far superior to anything that had been produced by the Germans. In 1947 the Three M Company began selling it commercially under the Scotch Tape trademark. This enormous advance was matched by tape recorder manufacturers, who were able to reduce the speed at which the tape passed under the recording head from 30 ips (inches per second) to 15 ips, and even 7½ ips, thus doubling and quadrupling the amount of recorded material stored on a reel of tape.

It came as no surprise to anyone that the broadcast and record companies snapped up tape recorders as soon as they were readily available. By 1948, 15-ips machines had been installed in every major record and radio studio throughout the country. The recorder's most appealing feature for radio was that it was virtually impossible for the listener to distinguish between a taped broadcast and a "live" broadcast. Mistakes made during broadcasts or recording sessions could be easily cut out of a tape and corrections inserted without the audience being any the wiser. The machine also eliminated the onerous studio chore of having to rerecord mistakes in three or four minute segments, the main drawback of the wax recording blank system. But the greatest advantage of the tape to recording companies was that it enabled producers to record complete movements of extended musical works or shorter musical pieces without interruption. This was an enormous improvement from the artistic standpoint.

Many record critics were convinced at the time that magnetic tapes would soon replace records in the home. They admitted that tape did have drawbacks: it became brittle and tended to break with age, and unless properly stored, it could become demagnetized. But the tape proponents were of the opinion that these disadvantages were far outweighed by the advantages of the new recording medium. With tape, there was no surface hiss, and the age-old problem of accidental needle scratch was solved. But most important, the tape medium made it possible for music lovers to hear recordings of symphonic works without the annoyance of changing record sides every four or five minutes.

These arguments for tape were sound. But those who were counting the disc out did not know that it was undergoing its own revolutionary changes behind the scenes. In fact, the grooved disc had not come even close to realizing its full potential and capabilities.

12

The Long-Playing Record

In April 1948, Ted Wallerstein of Columbia Records requested an appointment with David Sarnoff, the head of the vast Radio Corporation of America complex, which included the National Broadcasting Company and RCA Victor Records. Wallerstein stated that he had something of major importance to show to Sarnoff and any other key staff members he would care to invite. Soon after the meeting began, the attending representatives of the two arch-rivals arranged themselves around a conference table, the RCA men on one side, the Columbia men on the other. A small record player was quickly produced and hooked into a standard playback system. Wallerstein put a record on the turntable, started the motor, and placed the stylus in the outer groove. To the amazement of all the RCA men, the record played for twenty-three minutes without stopping, and the sound it produced was extremely good.

There was silence at the conclusion of the demonstration. The RCA executives knew that Wallerstein had brought off yet another coup. The long-playing record was at last a reality, and Columbia had won the laurels. Wallerstein, however, had not organized the meeting to flaunt Columbia's achievement. His purpose was to convince his chief competitor to adopt the new record medium. He went on to summarize for the group the features of the long-playing record.

The extensive playing time of the new disc had been achieved by reducing its speed from the standard 78 to 33⅓ revolutions per minute and by greatly increasing the number of grooves on its surface — from 85 per inch to 300 per inch, on the average. The 33⅓ speed had been used for years for sixteen-inch radio transcription discs. It was the lowest speed at which inexpensive electrical motors could operate efficiently and consistently — an important consideration when musical pitch is involved. Although Wallerstein did not dwell on the matter, the fact that Columbia engineers had been able to cut microgrooves without hampering the quality of the original recording was indeed a small miracle.

Another key to the success of the long-play record was contributed by engineers at Philco, a major radio and phonograph manufacturer: a light-weight pickup, or needle cartridge, and a tone arm that imposed only eight grams of pressure as it tracked the narrow grooves of the disc. The importance of this development cannot be minimized, since the new long-playing record was pressed on vinylite, an extremely soft plastic compound. The standard, heavy tone arm of the day would have worn out a vinylite record after only a few playings.

Wallerstein went on to say that he was convinced that

the public would abandon the 78 rpm record in favor of the long-playing record as soon as they learned of the new disc's many advantages. It offered music with very few breaks in continuity. For the first time, a record could play music much as it was heard in the concert hall. The new disc required far less storage space than did the standard shellac record. The vinylite long-play pressings were light and unbreakable, both highly attractive features. But the main advantage of the new record had to do with simple economics. Since the long-playing record could increase the playing time of an individual disc at least fivefold, it would most assuredly reduce the cost to the consumer of recorded entertainment — once, of course, he had invested in the necessary new equipment.

This was why, reasoned Wallerstein, it was so important that the entire industry act immediately to promote the long-play cause. Once the public accepted the new record, sales volume would unquestionably increase and there would be more than enough profits for all. To facilitate matters, Wallerstein offered to hand over to RCA Victor all of the research data and manufacturing specifications compiled by the Columbia Records and the Columbia Broadcasting System research staffs, who had worked on the development of the microgroove record jointly. He added that Columbia would make no attempt to collect patent fees or royalties. The long-playing record was to be free to all in the industry.

As the meeting drew to a close, David Sarnoff's positive attitude led several of the Columbia executives to believe that RCA Victor would join the crusade for the long-playing record. This was most heartening for the Columbia men, who foresaw that if this were to happen the record business would soar to heights hitherto unknown.

There was another, more concrete reason for Columbia to be anxious about Sarnoff's cooperation. The faster the new record was established, the more quickly Columbia could begin to recoup the substantial investment the company had made in the project, which dated back to the pre–World War II period.

The project had been undertaken soon after Wallerstein took over the reins at Columbia, following the label's acquisition by CBS. Recalling the unfulfilled promise of the long-playing record during his first months at RCA Victor, Wallerstein recommended that this concept be given a top research and development priority. Work had begun immediately, only to be postponed by the war. Experimentation resumed again in 1946, under the direction of two key men: Bill Bachman, the research director of Columbia Records; and Peter Goldmark, who had organized a research laboratory for CBS.

At first, there was some concern about what constituted a long-playing record side. How long did it have to play? After he had timed the major symphonic recordings, Wallerstein determined that virtually all of the great symphonies would fit on from one to four record sides if the playing time of a record side was twenty-eight minutes. This time capacity became the objective of the researchers. Finally, in September 1947, Bachman and Goldmark reported that they had achieved their goal.*

* The accomplishment was the result of team effort. Therefore it is sad to note that in various magazine and newspaper articles published in 1973, Peter Goldmark claims virtually all of the credit for the development of the long playing record. In fact, the concept of extending the playing time of a disc record goes back many pre-Goldmark years. Neo-

Although Sarnoff had indeed been impressed, weeks were to pass with no word of RCA Victor's decision. Wallerstein began to fret. He was reluctant to announce the long play to the public without RCA Victor's support, since several of his objectives had not as yet been reached. Against Wallerstein's better judgment, CBS president Frank Stanton, in an attempt to woo Philco's advertising away from NBC, had granted Philco exclusive rights to the production of long-playing record playback equipment. Wallerstein, anxious to establish the microgroove record as the industry standard, would have preferred that *all* phonograph manufacturers be given the specifications to make 33⅓ players. To further complicate matters for him, Philco was unable to design an automatic long-playing record changer capable of intermixing different sizes of records. Had this been accomplished early, it would have been a giant step in the direction of establishing the new record; and it would have discouraged anyone from challenging Columbia with an alternative to the long play.

More weeks went by without word from RCA. Wallerstein decided that he had better postpone the announcement of the long-playing disc. But Bill Paley, the chairman of the board at CBS, feared that further delay might allow a potential competitor the opportunity of announcing a similar development and thus stealing Columbia's thunder. He overruled Wallerstein.

---

phone, a British firm, tried it in 1906. As we have seen, Edison in a desperate attempt to revitalize his dying record company, attempted it in 1927. And it was actually Ted Wallerstein, at RCA Victor in 1932, who remembered its unfulfilled promise. In 1938 he recommended to CBS that it be a subject for research and development, some seven years before Goldmark says he first thought of it.

On June 21, 1948, Wallerstein formally announced the long-playing record to the press at a suit in the Waldorf Astoria Hotel in New York City. He proceeded to demonstrate the record with a Philco turntable attachment that could be "jacked," or plugged, into any radio or conventional phonograph player. The attachment, he mentioned, would retail for $29.95.

The results of the press conference were phenomenal. By the end of the year, and in spite of RCA Victor's continued silence, Columbia had sold 1,250,000 long-playing records. The public quickly recognized the advantages of the new disc, but the great success of Columbia's initial promotion was also due to the fact that a wide variety of musical fare had been offered in the new medium. This was made possible only because of Wallerstein's brilliant foresight.

Anticipating the long-playing record before it became a reality, Wallerstein had years ago instructed the Columbia Records engineering department to record simultaneously on 78 rpm wax recording blanks and sixteen-inch, 33⅓ rpm radio transcription blanks made of glass. Although the music recorded on the blanks was of necessity broken up into three- and four-minute segments, Wallerstein knew that, having been recorded at the correct speed and in sequence, these recorded performances could be easily transferred to long-playing records in the future. This meant Columbia would have an extensive catalogue of material ready for the new medium before its competitors had even dreamed of the possibility of long-playing records.

Now, at the famous June twenty-first press meeting, Columbia also announced that it would make its long-play manufacturing facilities available to its competitors, or, alternatively, it would lend technical assistance to other record companies deciding to establish their own long-play pressing facilities. Most of the record firms decided to defer making a decision until RCA Victor made a move. They did not have long to wait.

Early in 1949, word finally came from RCA Victor. The giant company had decided to spurn the Columbia long-playing record in favor of its own innovation — a seven-inch, microgroove, nonbreakable record designed to play at a completely new speed, 45 revolutions per minute. Like Columbia's long-playing record, Victor's 45 rpm disc would require a special turntable.

The record industry was utterly flabbergasted when word of the third speed spread. The RCA Victor record appeared to have little to recommend it over the 78, aside from being lighter, more durable and more easily stored. It most certainly did not play any longer than the average 78 side. The burning question at that moment was why RCA had decided to promote a record obviously less desirable than Columbia's 33⅓ long-playing record. The answer may never be made public, but it is assumed that RCA saw the 33⅓ long play as the last straw in a series of setbacks it had suffered in its rivalry with the "upstart" CBS organization. And indeed, the 33⅓ disc was to prove itself the bane of the RCA Victor Record Company, for here begins the battle of the speeds.

13

33⅓ or 45?

The public's reaction to these struggles within the industry was one of complete bewilderment. And it is axiomatic that when people are puzzled about what to buy, they usually do not buy anything. It looked as if, in all the confusion, the booming record trade would falter once again.

Nevertheless, RCA took pains to ensure the success of the 45. Millions of dollars were poured into a gigantic promotional and advertising campaign to launch 45 records and players. The machines were sold at prices close to actual cost to ensure a wide circulation.

RCA was also fortunate in winning the unexpected alliance of juke box machine manufacturers, who quickly saw the advantages of the smaller record for multiple selection machines. The large center hole of the 45 also opened up the possibility of great improvement in the design of automatic record selection devices.

As a result of its massive campaign, RCA did succeed

in selling a great many 45 machines — a task made easier by Columbia's failure to produce a record changer capable of handling records of different sizes.

But in spite of all of the RCA hoopla, a steadily increasing number of people converted to the long-playing record after coming to the conclusion that it was the better buy. It was apparent that music on 33⅓ was cheaper. A Tchaikovsky symphony on 78s sold for $7.28. Columbia was able to issue the symphony on a single long-playing record retailing for $4.85. Though the cost of music on 45 discs averaged about the same as the long-playing record, no one wanted to contend with changing record sides every three or four minutes. And storing a symphony or a complete opera on 45s was about as easy as trying to find space on a shelf for a small accordion.

In the summer of 1949, a number of the smaller record companies specializing in classical recordings, among them Vox Records and Cetra-Soria, decided in favor of the 33⅓ long play. Shortly thereafter, these pioneers were joined by Mercury, Decca and Capitol, although the latter company hedged its bets by releasing its new recordings both on 33⅓ and 45 discs. British Decca, which had separated from American Decca during the war, began releasing long-playing records in the United States under its newly established London Records trademark.

Much to Edward Wallerstein's chagrin, Columbia's European affiliate, the powerful E.M.I. group, decided not to convert to 33⅓ rpm. This gave the British Decca–London organization an enormous head start in the British Commonwealth countries.

As the war of the speeds dragged on, phonograph equipment manufacturers decided that discretion was the

Dr. Peter Goldmark, former head of CBS Laboratories, in a 1948 photo demonstrating the space-saving advantages of the 33⅓ microgroove record. All the music on the 78 rpm albums to his right is contained on the long-playing discs in his hands

better part of valor. Henceforth, all of the turntables and record changers now manufactured by neutral companies would be designed to play all three existing types of records. Although this was the practical course, the public was forced to pay the price — and still does for that matter. A three-speed turntable obviously costs more to manufacture than a single-speed turntable. *

The battle of the speeds continued until 1950, when RCA Victor grudgingly conceded defeat with an announcement that it would begin releasing 33⅓ long-playing records. By this time the company had reportedly lost millions of dollars in its attempt to establish the 45 rpm record as the prime record medium. But RCA would have probably continued to sustain financial losses to keep the fight alive, were it not for the fact that a number of Victor's most important artists threatened to quit if the company continued to balk at releasing their recordings on long-playing discs.

Columbia's triumph was only partial. Soon the 45, rather than the 33⅓, disc would become the ultimate medium for pop recordings. Wallerstein's hope for a one-speed industry had not come to pass. Following his retirement in 1951, Columbia began to issue pop recordings on 45s.

---

* Eventually a fourth speed, 16 rpm, was introduced by record player manufacturers to accommodate producers of recordings for the blind. Obviously, a 16 rpm record rotates at half the speed of a standard 33⅓ disc; this permits a blind person to listen to readings of extended literary works with relatively few side changes and for lower prices. Sixteen rpm records offering musical works have never been issued commercially, because mass produced, inexpensive home playback equipment is incapable of controlling pitch when operating at speeds lower than 33⅓ rpm.

The uneasy peace that followed these resolutions in the industry did much to clear the air for the average record fan. At least he knew that it was safe to buy classical, jazz, Broadway musical and popular album recordings in the long-play format without fear of the records becoming outmoded. The 45 rpm record was by now the pop single medium and little more.

Today, more than two decades after the war of the speeds, the triumph of the 33⅓ rpm long-playing record is even more dramatic. Only 15 percent of all the records sold in the United States are 45s, and many modern juke boxes play only 33⅓ records.

14

The Spawning of Independent Labels

During the 1950s, the recording industry experienced tremendous growth in a variety of ways. A rash of small independent record companies that specialized in classical music recording sprang up, among them Westminster, the Haydn Society, Vanguard and Vox. These companies, utilizing the tape recorder to the fullest advantage, produced orchestral and operatic works in Europe with lesser-known artists at costs considerably below those usually paid by the major American record companies. Since these so-called independent classical companies were able to maintain low operating costs, they could make profits on relatively modest sales. A number of these labels were encouraged enough to record musical compositions that were rarely heard — even in the concert hall — and known only to a handful of musicologists. Soon an enormous variety of recorded classical music was available to the public in the new long-play medium.

Besides these small classical labels, many small independent "pop" labels appeared in the fifties. These specialized in jazz, folk music, country and western, and rhythm and blues (the father of soul music). Many of them — Imperial, Atlantic, Chess, Checker, King, Folkways and others — are very much in existence today.

As a result of the expansion of these new companies and their stock, sales and distribution patterns of the record industry began to change. Record retailing in the old 78 rpm shellac era had been a fairly simple matter. The record dealer had had only a few labels to stock, and the fact that shellac records were heavy and fragile precluded the possibility of their being sold by mail. Now the average dealer found that he was no longer able to keep up with the tremendous outpouring of records from the new labels. To add to his woes, large discount stores, based primarily in New York, began to exploit the long-playing record's advantage as a mail-order commodity. These large stores, including Sam Goody and the Record Hunter, launched nationwide advertising campaigns, offering to deliver long-playing records anywhere, and at substantial discounts.

Most dealers realized that they would have to resort to selling records at discount in order to stay in business. But moving to a discount business forced dealers to give up certain time-honored fixtures: the listening booth, in which a customer could actually hear a record before buying it, was the first casualty in the discount revolution. Professional record clerks, who prided themselves on their knowledge of the merits of competing records, were considered expensive luxuries. Lastly, the profit squeeze forced the dealer to dispense with all his limited-demand or specialized interest records, even though they may have been of high artistic merit or cultural importance. He had to stick to sure-fire hits. Because of these factors, the record store evolved into a self-service operation with a check-out counter, not unlike a supermarket.

This trend in record retailing in turn backfired on the smaller classical record labels. Many fell prey to the demands of the big discount operations in New York, who promised the "big buy" if manufacturers would cut prices substantially. This tended to accelerate the spread of self-service discount retailing; but the smaller labels depended as much upon the full list price "catalogue" dealers throughout the country as they did upon the New York discount houses. As discounting spread, most of the independent classical labels experienced severe financial problems. Those that survived did so either by selling records at budget prices, or by diversifying their musical fare. Some were bought out by larger companies. But perhaps the greatest factor in prolonging their lives was a phenomenon called "high fidelity."

Prior to the 1950s, most of the record players in American homes had been radio-phonograph combinations with limited dynamic range. This continued to be the case in the early fifties, even though it was common knowledge that enormous progress had been made in electronics during World War II. The major phonograph and radio manufacturers were convinced that the American public preferred the muddled tonal quality common in recorded music at the time, with mellow highs and booming, tubby-sounding bass. A statistical survey taken at the time of the introduction of FM broadcasting seemed to bear out their conviction. It reported that only one family in four preferred static-free, full-range radio reproduction to the usual sounds heard on AM radio.

But the record-buying public was soon to change its taste in sound. Early in the war, British Decca engineers had developed a recording system so sensitive that it could detect the differences in sounds between British and German submarines. The system was applied to musical recording in 1944. After the war, full frequency range recordings (ffrr) were released on British Decca's American label, London Records.

The ffrr records were a sensation on the English and American markets. It was not long before most of the progressive American companies were also producing wide-range, or high-fidelity, recordings of comparable quality. This, in turn, triggered a demand for more sensitive playback equipment.

The demand was not satisfied by the manufacturers of orthodox phonograph consoles or table models, who continued to offer their standard wares under long-established brand names and trademarks. Rather, a new breed of smaller companies grew up, specializing in the manufacture of high-quality parts, or "components," of the audio system: needle cartridges (pickups), amplifiers, speakers and turntables. Thus the audio enthusiast could assemble a playback system tailored to his own taste. The "component" manufacturers also produced a device called a "preamplifier." This became a necessary addition to many component systems with the widespread use of General Electric's variable reluctance magnetic needle cartridge — an efficient and inexpensive unit. Because of the low voltage output of the G.E. cartridge, an intermediate step-up in power was needed before the electrical impulses could be relayed from the cartridge to the amplifier. The additional power source was provided by the preamplifier. The G.E. pickup was the first cartridge of high quality to be mass-produced, and its widespread use did a great deal to enhance the sound of both records and equipment.

By 1954, high-fidelity shows, at which component manufacturers loudly demonstrated their wares, were being held in virtually every major city. The fans who bought the equipment and attended the shows were a relatively small but extremely passionate group of people who had discovered a new and exciting hobby: the quest for accuracy in sound reproduction. To the trade they were known as the lunatic fringe. To the public, they were known as "hi-fi bugs." And for some inexplicable reason, they were almost invariably male.

In every other respect a normal human being, the hi-fi bug developed an unquenchable passion for tweeters (a special addition to a speaker, designed to emphasize high frequencies) and woofers (to reproduce low frequencies); and he was more than ready to come to blows in defense of a favorite pickup or amplifier. Though hi-fi bugs were never large in number, even among record buyers, they exerted a great deal of influence on an impressionable public. The major phonograph manufacturers found it to their advantage to jump on the hi-fi bandwagon with talk of special tweeters and woofers. Record companies found it difficult to sell records not clearly labeled "high fidelity." Not a few companies had hi-fi stickers pasted on old record jackets. The man in the street began to refer to his record player as "my hi-fi set," just as his father had called any kind of playback machine a Victrola.

But the hi-fi craze was destined to be relatively short. Before the end of the 1950s, a new word entered the lexicon of the world of sound — "stereo."

15

"Booze, Broads and Payola"

Before we consider the stereo era in the history of recording, other developments in the industry should be reviewed.

In the early 1950s the structure of the entertainment world was shattered by the impact of television. This powerful new medium wreaked financial havoc with most other forms of entertainment, but the record business was one of the exceptions. The two media complemented rather than competed with each other. While music and sound were the lifeblood of the record business, television offered very little musical programming; and the quality of sound produced by the average television set left much to be desired.

The effect of television on radio and motion pictures was another matter. Hollywood was particularly hard hit. Milton Berle, Sid Caesar and the other major TV stars of the era turned movie house box offices into depressed areas, particularly those that had thrived on the run-of-the-mill offerings of the big Hollywood film factories. To this day, a much smaller but more innovative motion picture industry is still trying to find a way to cope with the television medium.

Television's effect on radio was equally devastating, although the outcome for radio was far happier than it was for the film industry.

The top radio stations of the 1940s had sustained high listener ratings and proportionately high advertising revenues by broadcasting popular network shows, most of which emanated from either New York or Los Angeles. The shows ranged from "prime time" regulars, like Duffy's Tavern and the Kraft Music Hall, to a seemingly endless succession of afternoon soap operas; John's Other Wife, Back Stage Wife and Stella Dallas were typical examples. The time between the afternoon "soapers" (as they were called in the radio trade) and the big coast-to-coast shows was filled with syndicated children's shows such as Buck Rogers in the 25th Century, The Lone Ranger, and Jack Armstrong, the All-American Boy.

The mercurial rise of television prompted the major radio sponsors to divert the main part of their advertising appropriations from radio to the new medium. It was not long before all radio network shows, even those featuring personalities of the caliber and popularity of Fred Allen, Edgar Bergen and Charlie McCarthy, W. C. Fields, Ed Wynn and Bing Crosby, joined the cigar store Indian as beloved but nearly forgotten landmarks in the American past.

Now the leading radio stations found themselves deprived of advertising income and without either the expertise or the means of producing their own programs.

This predicament led radio broadcasters to turn to a new and even more lucrative source of program material: recorded music.

The disc jockey show was not a new development. Even in the midst of the golden days of big-time radio, a growing number of radio stations had tried out the "Make Believe Ballroom" program formula with enormous success. Some stations had adopted the deejay show to provide their audiences with better listening fare than the dreary run of soap operas. But more often broadcasters had resorted to "canned" music out of economic necessity.

By 1950, the tail was wagging the dog, as virtually every radio station in the country began devoting all or most of its broadcast day to recorded music. At the time, it was a happy wedding. The record companies, anxious to have radio stations promote their records, either sold the stations records at nominal costs or, very often, gave the records to the stations for nothing. Radio provided the record business with a nationwide auditioning booth; the record business provided radio with the means to reap windfall profits.

The music publishing fraternity, the famous residents of Tin Pan Alley, quickly realized that the record business had acquired new influence — both esthetically and economically. Not only did the record companies control all the music offered on discs, they now provided most of the music programmed on radio. Radio exposure stimulated record sales, increasing the music publisher's income at the rate of 2 cents per tune per record sold (which the publisher traditionally split with the composers and lyric writers). Of equal importance to the publisher was the income he derived from the actual broadcasting of the music. Although artists and record companies to this day do not receive fees for broadcasts of their recorded performances, music publishers do.

Suddenly the record producer, or "artist and repertoire" man, became a kingmaker in the eyes of the music publisher. The successful A&R men of the era became known in the music trade as "the knights of the round table." They decided what songs to record, who should record them, and how each song was to be treated. They also selected arrangers and orchestrators, side musicians and singers.

There is good reason to believe that, beginning in the early fifties, unscrupulous publishers were not above attempting to bribe A&R men to favor their tunes over those of competing publishers. There is equally good reason to believe that some of the more venal A&R men succumbed to their offers. One of the more popular forms of reward was to give a cooperative A&R man a "piece," or a share, of a song with no hit potential. The song could then be recorded and issued on the "B" side of a 45 with a sure-fire hit recording on the "A" side. Copyright owners of the songs on both sides of a record earn the same royalties.

No matter what form a reward took — cash, an ocean cruise, a share in the copyright, a case of whiskey at Christmas — gifts from publishers became known in the record business as "payola." Bribery was, of course, not unknown in the record trade, even back in the cylinder days. But it had never been as rampant as it was to become in the mid-fifties.

The disease spread rapidly to hundreds of radio stations, particularly those specializing in teen-age music. Influential disc jockeys who enjoyed large listening audiences on radio or television became the prime targets of a group of publisher contact men, and promotion men working for record companies and distributors.

It was no secret that some radio station owners were not overly generous when it came to paying disc jockeys their salaries, preferring that they supplement their incomes in other ways. Consequently, a rather large number of deejays felt no compunctions about demanding money or gifts from the swarm of promotion men who hovered about them, in exchange for plugging selected records on the air.

Payola developed into a dirty business. Under federal law, radio and television broadcasters are deemed holders of the public trust. Therefore, the acceptance of a bribe to influence program content is legally a violation of that trust. Yet when the term "payola" was widely used in the record and radio trades during the fifties, not a few radio station executives chose to ignore the situation. Those who decided to take steps to solve the dilemma found an ingenious solution — the "Top Hit Playlist."

Whether a station adopted the Top Forty or Top Fifty format, the object was the same. By playing only the hottest records, based exclusively on local surveys of retail sales or on national best-seller charts, a station would maintain high listener ratings and thus be in a position to demand top advertising rates; meanwhile, the power of disc jockeys would be severely curtailed.

The "Top Forty" solution was received with little enthusiasm by astute record executives. As more and more stations adopted the formula, hit records became overexposed and less air time was available for new records and their artists. The time allocated to the exposure of selected new records ("picks") fell under the control of radio station program directors or "big personality" jockeys. Competition for the limited number of open time slots threw record promotion men into a frenzy. Stakes were higher than ever before, and consequently payola increased rather than decreased.

The situation reached its climax at the infamous national disc jockey convention held in Miami Beach in the spring of 1959. Publishers and record men engaged in a wild competition to win the favors of disc jockeys by plying them with sumptuous meals, gallons of expensive liquor, and even high-priced prostitutes. The convention turned out to be a colossal orgy, said to rival the legendary orgies of ancient Rome.

Soon after, *Time* magazine reported in graphic terms the juicier aspects of the convention under the headline "Booze, Broads and Payola."

The article created a national scandal. Within months, government investigating committees were holding hearings in key cities throughout the country. Disc jockeys, program directors, radio station owners, record distribution executives and promotion men were called to testify. A number of the witnesses were forced to acknowledge damaging evidence of their involvement with payola; others, under oath, freely admitted their complicity. All were granted amnesty after swearing that they would not engage in payola in the future.

The scandal produced a stringent federal antipayola law and today, for the most part, the malaise has been stamped out. It is now a common, and legal, practice for record companies to pay for radio time and advertising announcements to promote records. This way, record companies are assured of having their music broadcast, and probably at a lower cost than the old, indirect payola method.

Yet record men who are "in the know" will admit in confidence that payola still persists to a certain degree. Most recently, a new scandal in the industry seems to have borne this out.

In the spring of 1973, the industry was rocked by the news that Clive Davis, the president of CBS/Columbia Records considered by many to be the top executive in the trade, was fired for allegedly misappropriating corporate funds for his personal use. Two of Davis's aides were also accused of embezzlement. One of them, David Wynshaw, subsequently testified before a Senate crime strike force committee in Newark, New Jersey. According to newspaper accounts, Wynshaw told the committee that CBS Records and other recording firms were heavily involved in payola, particularly with the black disc jockey fraternity. CBS officials vehemently denied the allegation, claiming that Wynshaw was not in a position to speak with authority since he was not directly engaged in radio station promotion. Nevertheless, subsequent newspaper articles have indicated that the committee in Newark and other Senate investigators are not taking the charges lightly. Some further reports have alluded to the fact that hard drug fixes are sometimes arranged by recording officials in lieu of cash payments to jockeys. Thus an ugly new industry term has been coined, "drugola."

Up until the publication of the famous *Time* article that exposed the payola scandal of the fifties, the general public had been unaware of what had been taking place behind the scenes. As far as most record fans were concerned, recordings were better than ever. Pop vocalists, both male and female, continued to dominate the best-seller charts. Many of them achieved stardom in the late forties and early fifties. Among these were Perry Como, Eddy Fisher, Frankie Laine, Tony Bennett, Rosemary Clooney, Doris Day, Patti Page and Frank Sinatra. Sinatra, after being dropped from the artist roster of Columbia Records and, apparently, from the public's favor, staged an impressive comeback at Capitol Records, adding impetus to the rapid growth of the young Hollywood-based company. Not a small part of the success of the Sinatra revival was due to brilliant orchestral arrangements provided by Nelson Riddle.

A group of sensational young artists reached top stardom in the latter half of the decade. Pat Boone came close to breaking all-time best-selling marks with his recording of "Love Letters in the Sand." A recording of "Autumn Leaves" catapulted pianist Roger Williams to international popularity. The Everly Brothers reached the zenith of their career with a tune called "All I Have To Do Is Dream." Bobby Darin with "Mack the Knife" and Paul Anka with "Lonely Boy" were responsible for other hits of the fifties. Also during these years, a host of black artists rose to the forefront of the recording industry, equaling, and in many cases, surpassing white artists in popularity. Nat "King" Cole, Johnnie Mathis, Roy Hamilton, Sarah Vaughn, Diahann Carroll, Tommy Edwards, Mahalia Jackson, the Platters, Little Richard and Gloria Lynn are only a few names on a long and impressive list.

Broadway musicals of the fifties were another source

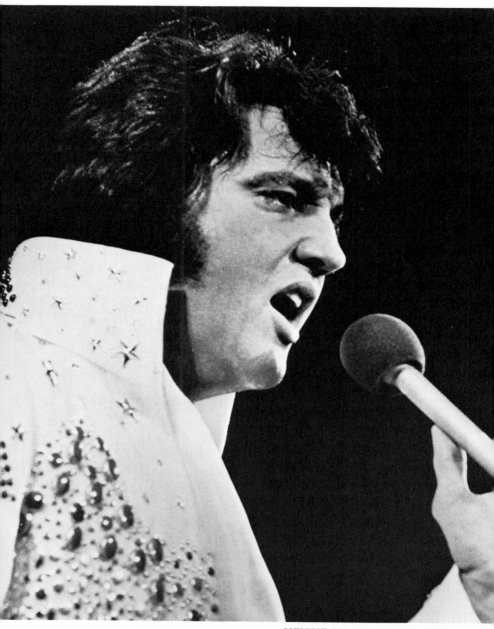

Elvis Presley

of hit singles and albums. The most notable show, of course, was the Lerner and Loewe production of *My Fair Lady*, starring Rex Harrison and Julie Andrews. The sale of original cast albums combined with other recordings of songs from the show numbered in the tens of millions. Lerner and Loewe's *Camelot*, again starring Julie Andrews, this time with Richard Burton, was another tremendous boon to the record industry. But perhaps the most notable Broadway production of the decade was *West Side Story*, with music by Leonard Bernstein and lyrics by Stephen Sondheim. The production was highly innovative and original in concept, and represented a significant departure from Broadway musicals of the past.

But the most representative figure in the record business for that decade has to have been Elvis Presley. The gyrating young singing sensation from Tennessee created an entirely new entertainment form by combining two popular styles: country and western and rock 'n' roll. Presley racked up hit record after hit record in a seemingly endless succession. His outstanding sellers were "All Shook Up" and "Don't Be Cruel."

Rock 'n' roll evolved from musical forms created by black musicians, and began gathering momentum in the mid-fifties. Ironically, as with early jazz recordings, the first artists to exploit the new trend were white. Bill Haley and His Comets' "Rock Around the Clock" was a sensational hit both in the United States and abroad. But at the crest of the rock 'n' roll craze was a black artist named Chubby Checker. His recording of "The Twist" ranks as the greatest single record to date, both in terms of the total number of records it sold and the length of time it remained popular: "The Twist" was on the Top Ten best-seller charts for three consecutive years. No succeeding recording artists, not even the Beatles, have come close to Checker's mark.

16

The Age of Stereo

THE 1950s introduced a period of undreamed of expansion in the music business. But the industry did not stop to rest on its laurels as it had done during previous periods of prosperity. Record men knew that the possibilities for continued growth were limitless. This conviction, which seemed to prevail throughout the industry, inspired further innovation as well as the implementation of new recording methods and techniques. The hi-fi era had scarcely reached its peak when stereo records were introduced in 1958.

The art of stereophony has a longer history than most people realize. Stereophonic experimentation began as soon as scientists recognized that a monaural playback system was incapable of producing a three-dimensional effect in sound; this was clearly because, with a monaural system, the recorded sounds emanated from one source, namely, the loudspeaker.

Students of sound know that a person with two good

ears hears quite differently than a person with only one good ear. Those of us who are fortunate enough to possess two good ears can readily locate the sources of the sounds we hear. Also, the sounds we hear seem "round," or three-dimensional. This effect is called a psychoacoustic phenomenon. Contemporary scientists are still at odds with one another about explaining this miracle.

Early experimenters in stereophonic sound fashioned models of human heads, in which microphones were substituted for ears. The sounds picked up by each microphone were relayed separately by wire directly to headphones. The listener wearing the headphones would hear the stereophonic effect as though he were actually sitting in the studio. Next came the discovery that both channels could be recorded and replayed through headphones, thus re-creating sound stereophonically. These early experiments, although successful, were put to no practical application, since mandatory headphones were considered a nuisance. Scientists then began to experiment with ways to create the stereophonic effect with multiple microphones and loudspeakers.

The first significant breakthrough in stereophony was made in 1931 by a scientist named Blumlein. While employed at the laboratories of English Columbia, he developed a system capable of producing the stereophonic effect using two microphones and two speakers. Blumlein discovered that the key element in creating the three-dimensional effect was the placement of the speakers during the playback phase. To obtain the best results, he discovered that the speakers, each producing separately recorded signals, should be placed at right angles to each other and about ten feet apart. If the listener placed himself at right angles to the speakers and at a point equidistant from them, his right ear heard the sound picked up by the right-hand microphone, and reproduced through the right-hand speaker, and his left ear picked up the sound generated by the left-hand microphone and speaker. The result was true stereophony.

Blumlein subsequently suggested methods of recording stereophonically on discs. His first approach was to cut each recorded channel in separate grooves. Thus two sets of grooves would appear on the surface of the record — side by side. This system required a pair of matching amplifiers and speakers, and, of course, twin styluses and cartridges. Naturally, the system was costly, but its greatest drawback was that, by requiring double the number of grooves, it reduced the playing time of a record by half.

The public's reaction to Blumlein's invention was almost complete indifference. But then Blumlein came up with a second proposal that had vast appeal: the signals from the two channels would be recorded in the same record groove, thus requiring only one cartridge and stylus. Although Blumlein never quite took this suggestion beyond the idea stage, his thinking did stimulate other scientists in the years following. Gradually, through a pooling of effort and information, recording engineers evolved the 45/45 stereo recording system, in common use today.

It operates as follows:

The stereo recording stylus is mounted at forty-five degree angles to the two walls of the record groove, and is suspended in such a way that it can vibrate both laterally and up and down. It is in turn connected by rods to moving coil vibrators so that the two channels of sound are recorded simultaneously on both walls of the record groove. The sound from the left-hand microphone drives the right-hand rod, making it fluctuate, which in turn causes the left side of the cutting stylus to cut a track into the left, or inner, side of the groove wall. Signals originating in the right-hand microphone cause the left-hand rod to vibrate, which in turn is reflected by recording stylus tracks on the right, or outer, groove wall.

Without going into great technical detail, stereo playback systems work in much the same way, only in reverse. The playback stylus picks up the sounds of the two channels traced into the inner and outer groove walls. These are transmitted by the cartridge to the stereo amplifier, which in fact is comprised of two matching amplifiers within the same housing. The amplified signals are then relayed to the twin speakers.

This stereo system was finally perfected in the mid-fifties. Phonograph equipment manufacturers were eager to promote it, even if it meant the obsolescence of the monaural sets already in use. They realized that stereo would ultimately yield higher profits because of its twin speaker and amplifier requirements.

The major record companies were far less enthusiastic about the prospect of stereo records. Most of them were somewhat embarrassed, because few stereo recording sessions had taken place before the mid-fifties, and so they had few stereo recordings to offer the public. Then there was that nagging fear that the millions of dollars that the major firms had invested in monaural recordings might soon be rendered worthless by the new multichannel recording technique.

But the new system was not to be denied. Smaller record companies with less monaural inventory to lose decided to get a head start on their giant competitors. They began issuing a flood of stereo records aimed at the hi-fi bug's younger brother, the stereophile. Most of these were known to the trade as "gimmick" or "ping-pong" records, because they seemed to send sound bouncing back and forth between the two speakers. Few of them were produced to display the less spectacular but far more important virtues of stereophony: a sense of realism, depth and spaciousness. Nor did they yet demonstrate the fact that the sound from two speakers driven by a relatively inexpensive stereo amplifier seemed superior to the sound produced by the most expensive monaural system.

It was only a matter of months before stereo became the "in" system for the audiophile, and the term "hi-fi" quickly faded from the language. Record players were now referred to as "stereos," whether or not they were capable of reproducing the stereo effect.

Stereo was yet another triumph for the venerable disc record. Although by now seventy-five years of age, it had proved its versatility, and its possibilities still seemed limitless.

The commercial sale of prerecorded tapes had not fared nearly so well as discs. The cost of tape decks tended to be high and the cost of prerecorded tapes themselves had always been exorbitant in comparison to record prices. In 1959, the Ampex Company launched a campaign to establish a commercial tape market with the introduction of its stereo tape deck. The machine accommodated a four-track tape threaded between seven-inch reels. The surface of each tape was divided into four channels, or tracks. Two tracks recorded and played back as the tape was run in the forward direction; the other set of tracks functioned when the tape was reversed. This four-track system was a significant step by Ampex to bring the cost of tape within range of the cost of records, but it still suffered from one serious drawback — the onerous task of threading tapes from one reel to another.

Soon afterward tape research men solved that problem with the introduction of tape cartridges. The two most popular forms today are eight-track stereo cartridges, and cassettes.

The eight-track stereo cartridge houses a one-quarter-inch continuous loop tape that is lubricated to prevent breakage. When the cartridge is played, the tape unwinds from the spool, passes under the playback heads, and then is returned to the spool. An important feature of the eight-track cartridge is that the playback heads move automatically from one set of tracks to the next.

The cassette is a small reel-to-reel cartridge that utilizes unlubricated tape, one-eighth of an inch wide. The tape is divided into two or four tracks, depending on whether it is stereo or monaural. Stereo cassettes work on exactly the same principle that four-track stereo reel-to-reel tape does, except that threading is eliminated. The cassette automatically stops itself when the forward reel is fully unwound. The cassette cartridge is then removed and reinserted into the player, so that the take-up spool is in the forward play position, thereby allowing the other two channels on the surface of the tape to pass under the playback heads.

Tape cartridges have been heavily promoted by the

Three types of commercial tape products. From right, lower half of photo: four-track reel-to-reel; eight-track continuous loop cartridge; and cassette

automobile industry as the ideal medium for in-car entertainment. Since eight-track playback units are relatively inexpensive and may be jacked into stereo systems already in the home, the eight-track cartridge is a versatile and extremely popular variety of recorded tape product.

Until most recently, sales of cassettes have lagged considerably behind those of the eight-track cartridge. In some cases recordings on the thin tape used in cassettes have been inferior to those on eight-track tape. Also, the reel-to-reel configuration of the cassette makes it difficult to find a specific band of music, while the eight-track cartridge makes the task a relatively simple one. But in spite of these inherent disadvantages, the cassette is already firmly rooted in the educational equipment market; and its overall success in the recorded entertainment market increases daily, as it remains the cheapest, least fragile, and most portable form of tape cartridge.

The trend toward cassettes has been accelerated lately by the introduction of greatly improved narrow-gauge magnetic tape for commercial use and by the widespread use of the Dolby system. This system is a special electronic technique used in tape duplication that virtually eliminates all extraneous noises. The great improvement in the quality of sound reproduction of "Dolby-ized" cassettes indicates that this cartridge style may be the prerecorded tape medium of the future.

While tape sales in general have shown enormous growth in the past few years, the sale of records has increased at virtually the same rate. A large segment of the public continues to prefer the disc, and with good reason.

The cost of the materials used in a tape cartridge is much higher than that of the materials used in a record pressing. But many audiophiles prefer disc to tape for reasons other than economy. As already mentioned, should the tape in a cartridge break or become tangled, the damage is irreparable; but of even greater importance is the fact that a well-mastered and pressed disc is actually superior in sound quality to the general run of tape cartridges. If record technology continues to keep pace as it has in the past, it is difficult to imagine a time when disc recording will be outmoded by the tape cartridge.

17

Creating in the Studio

MULTITRACK TAPES have had a far greater impact on the recording studio than they have had on the consumer market.

In the early days of magnetic tape recording, recording engineers discovered that singers or instrumental soloists who worked slowly under studio conditions, or who were prone to frequent mistakes, could be recorded much more efficiently and economically through a process called "over dubbing." In order to avoid keeping musicians on hand in the studio while the singer or soloist struggled to make the right takes, the wise producer learned to record the orchestral accompaniments separately. The artist, whether a singer or a solo instrumentalist, could then be brought to the studio, where, with the aid of earphones, he could sing or perform along with the tape of the orchestral track. Next, both the prerecorded track and the newly recorded track were combined on a single tape.

It followed that the innovative producer could take the process one, two, or even three steps further, by having the vocalist or musician record "over" himself several times, either in unison or in harmony with previously recorded tracks. The record fan could then be treated to the experience of hearing a chorus of Rosemary Clooneys rather than just one Rosemary Clooney.

Next, audio engineers working with magnetic tape produced reverberation machines that were able to create the effect of echoes electronically. The typical reverberation machine divides recorded signals into two channels. The first signal is fed directly to the output amplifier. The second signal is recorded onto a continuous loop tape and is then rerecorded onto the tape carrying the first signal by means of a series of playback heads. Since these second signals arrive at the output amplifier just after the first ones, the mixture of the signals creates the illusion of echo. The amount of echo can be controlled by adjusting sound levels.

The introduction of stereo in the late 1950s stimulated even greater electronic experimentation. At first two microphones were used at recording sessions, but the number was increased to three when record producers discovered that a centrally located microphone enhanced the final stereo effect. Additional "accent mikes" were introduced to pick up or emphasize individual instruments within the orchestral fabric. As the craze for stereo separation mounted, the need for individual microphones for each section of an orchestra or band arose. By the early 1960s it was no longer uncommon to have sixteen or more microphones in use at a recording session.

Fortunately, tape capacities have kept pace with these

A modern recording studio

developments, and indeed made them possible. Modern record producers have the option of recording a session on two, four, eight, sixteen or thirty-two channels. However, whatever the number of tracks used, all tracks must ultimately be reduced to two channels to accommodate stereo records and prerecorded tapes. This occurs at the so-called mixing stage of recording. It is at this juncture that the producer can, in a sense, play god.

By manipulating four, eight or more tracks, by raising or lowering sound levels, by fading tracks in and out, by adding reverberation, and by using other electronic gimmicks, the producer rather than the artist can become the creative force behind a recording. Of course, the sounds the producer concocts in the studio cannot be re-created elsewhere; certainly not at a live performance in front of an audience.

A number of highly creative major artists who have written their own material, including members of the Beatles and Paul Simon of Simon and Garfunkel, realized some years ago that the giant multichanneled recording studio console was a creative instrument. As a result of their success, the studio is today considered by many artists the ideal environment in which to create. Arrangements are worked out, and at times whole songs are composed, during recording sessions. Record executives used to calculate that the average pop record album could be recorded in about nine hours. Today, they concede that nine months is a more realistic estimate. Recording costs have, consequently, risen astronomically. Nevertheless, the practice is bound to continue as long as the artists and groups who compose in the studio continue to sell large quantities of records.

The Beatles, certainly the best-known recording artists to emerge in the last decade, are prime examples of this trend. Beatlemania struck the United States in the early part of 1964. It did not come without warning. The Liverpool quartet had already made a name for themselves in England and on the Continent. In the United States, exposure on Jack Paar's and Ed Sullivan's television shows was all that was needed to launch their first Capitol single release, "I Want To Hold Your Hand." Ninety days later, at the end of March, the record had rocketed to the top of every best-seller chart in the United States. Sales reached an awe-inspiring 3,000,000 copies, far exceeding Capitol's previous best-selling singles: "Sixteen Tons" by Tennessee Ernie Ford, and the Kingston Trio's recording of "Tom Dooley." To no one's surprise, "Meet the Beatles," the group's first album, actually outsold their single release, reaching the 3,365,000 mark during the same ninety-day period.

The Beatles proceeded to turn out a seemingly endless succession of hit singles and albums of astounding variety: socially significant songs, humorous songs, songs based on drug-induced fantasies, and old-fashioned love songs. As they worked, they became increasingly adept at using recording studio wizardry and exotic instruments to create unique musical effects. Perhaps the culmination of this development was reached in the "Sergeant Pepper" album, a true studio creation and a stellar example of the new status gained by records in the world of entertainment. As one commentator on the record scene has astutely noted, "The record is the song." Today recording can do more than simply mirror the voice or a musical instrument; it has evolved as a true art form for which up to thirty-two tape channels have become the recording artist's palette.

Today the repertoire offered on records is varied and ranges from the highly complex to the very simple; from recordings of intricate scores by the contemporary composer Berio, who freely mixes standard symphonic instrumentation and choral parts with synthesizer music, to recordings of a folk singer accompanying himself on solo guitar.

Marshall McLuhan has pointed out that new communications media never replace older, established media. Radio did not replace newspapers or records; nor has television replaced radio or books. Each time, we end up simply having more media than we did before. The same applies to music. New musical combinations like jazz rock, as exemplified in the music of Blood, Sweat and Tears, or like country and blues by Credence Clearwater Revival, never really supplant older forms. There is a real and an easily traced connection between the Dust Bowl Ballads of Woody Guthrie and the modern songs of Bob Dylan. Comic stories have sold well on records from the days of Russell Hunting up to today's Bill Cosby. Bach compositions played on Robert Moog's synthesizer have been a sensation, yet people will always listen to the music of Bach performed on the instruments for which the music was originally intended. The clever, sophisticated music of Burt Bacharach is reminiscent of the brilliant songs of Cole Porter of twenty and thirty years ago.

In short, the modern record business is a wonderful amalgamation of old forms and new. It embraces the simple and the complex. It has evolved into an extremely important cultural medium. More new music is written

Blood, Sweat and Tears

specifically for recordings than for any other type of entertainment.

It should also be pointed out that the quality of contemporary recorded music is, generally speaking, far superior to the popular tunes that were offered to the public twenty or thirty years ago. The songs of Bob Dylan, John Hartford, Jimmy Webb and other modern writers are in dramatic contrast to the "June, moon and spoon" songs that flourished until the 1950s. Prominent modern groups — Santana; Blood, Sweat and Tears; the

161

Yes; the Band; Crosby, Stills, Nash and Young; Emerson, Lake and Palmer; and others — have ingeniously blended diverse musical forms, including classical, rock, folk, country and jazz, into new and innovative kinds of music. In a very real sense they have created new forms out of old patterns.

It is thus not surprising that young music fans have not abandoned popular music for more sophisticated types of music such as jazz, opera, chamber or symphonic music as their parents did. Modern popular music is now a meaningful and sophisticated art form. Furthermore, the more traditional fields of music have remained more or less static for the past twenty years. This is particularly true of classical music. Few "serious" modern compositions have made any noticeable impression on the public. Unfortunately, most composers of "serious" music today seem to be far more interested in the purely technical aspects of music composition than they are in pleasing record buyers or audiences in concert halls. Financial support from well-meaning foundations and jobs on the faculties of colleges and universities have freed many composers from the necessity of compromising their art in order to make a living; but they have also kept these composers isolated and without the incentive to write music which will have meaning for a great many people.

It is regrettable that the pop music field seems to be the only arena in which healthy innovation is taking place. But fortunately it is innovation with strong international flavoring. The Beatles were the vanguard of a powerful British movement. They were followed by the Dave Clark Five, Donovan, Tom Jones, Lulu, Petula Clark, the Rolling Stones, Joe Cocker, the Who, the

COURTESY DECCA/LONDON RECORDS

The Rolling Stones

Moody Blues and a host of others. Brazilian songwriters have greatly influenced American musical styles with a stream of superb songs, among which are "The Girl from Ipanema," "One Note Samba," and "Quiet Night of Quiet Stars." There have also been popular songs from Europe — "A Man and a Woman" and "Love is Blue," to mention only two.

What now of the future?

True to form, the record industry is entering another period of transition. The latest harbinger of change is the four-channel home playback system.

18

Anyone for Surround Sound?

THE LATEST BRAINCHILD of audio equipment manufacturers, with a strong assist from several record companies, has been variously named: quadrasonic, quadra-
phonic, quadrafonic, psychoacoustical, quadradial, or
simply quad. Whatever its name, it amounts to a playback
system for the home that reproduces four channels of
sound rather than stereo's two.

The new multichannel system is designed to give the
listener the illusion of greater sonic spaciousness, depth,
and realism than ever before. During a live orchestral
performance, the human ear hears the musical sounds
emanating from the stage, as well as the sounds reflected
from the sides and the back of the concert hall. The
reflected sounds reach the ear at lower intensities and at
slightly delayed intervals from the sounds reaching it
directly from the stage. The cumulative effect of the
direct and echoed sounds as they are relayed to the brain
is three-dimensional.

In the mid-1960s, a number of audio scientists, the majority of them Japanese, decided that the two-speaker, two-channel stereo system would never be capable of accurately re-creating this psychoacoustical phenomenon in the home environment. Their solution was to design a four-channel, four-speaker system. To appreciate it, the listener is required to seat himself in the center of the room in which the system is installed, with two speakers in front of him and two speakers to his rear. The two front speakers transmit the direct sounds of an orchestra, group, or solo performer. The two rear speakers transmit the reflected sounds. The result, to coin an old phrase, is concert hall realism.

Quad playback equipment and prerecorded tapes and discs are now available in retail shops. But the dedicated audiophile who may decide to install the new system in his living room will confront a dilemma. Equipment manufacturers and record companies are promoting two distinctly different kinds of quadrasonic systems: the discrete and the matrix.

According to some experts, the discrete system yields a better sound reproduction. During a discrete recording session, four separate microphones feed sound signals through four separate amplifier units. The amplified signals are then relayed to four distinct tape recording heads that transfer them to a four-track tape.

For home consumption, discrete recordings may be obtained in prerecorded tape cartridges or on discs.

In order to play a discrete cartridge, one must own a four-track tape player, four amplifier units and four speakers. If one prefers the discrete disc, it is necessary to buy a specially designed pickup cartridge and a demodulator, in addition to the proper amplifier and speakers. The disc itself registers the four channels of sound in a single groove. Two channels are recorded on each groove wall, which, like the standard stereo disc, is cut at an angle of forty-five degrees to the surface of the record. The discrete disc is also playable on standard stereo playback equipment, though only the two channels directed to the front two speakers can be faithfully reproduced in stereo.

The matrix system also utilizes four channels of sound. However, during the recording phase, the four channels are mixed, or "encoded," into two channels. Thus, when a matrix recording is played back, the sound must be separated into four channels again before being transmitted to the four amplifier and speaker units. This electronic miracle is accomplished by a device called a decoder, or quad simulator.

The advantage of the matrix system is that the decoder unit can be fully adapted to regular stereo equipment, with, of course, the addition of two extra amplifiers and speakers. The matrix, or "SQ" (stereo-quad), disc is also completely compatible with regular stereo equipment, since it retains in its grooves the two basic stereo modulations for the right and left front speakers.

The illusion of concert hall realism created by quad playback systems has so far been applied mostly to classical recordings and recordings of large popular orchestral arrangements. On the other hand, producers of smaller pop bands and rock groups have experimented with quad by splitting their musicians into four sections, each with its own tape channel. Hearing these recordings played back through equidistant speakers gives the listener the

A modern playback unit designed for the home, capable of reproducing the sound contained on stereo or stereo-quad records, eight-track tape cartridges and standard, two- or four-channel radio broadcasts

effect of being right in the middle of the band rather than in the audience.

It will be interesting to learn the fate of quad recording, and not only from the standpoint of finding out which system — discrete or matrix — eventually prevails. At the moment either system is far more expensive than comparable stereo equipment. But more crucial to the success of quad is the listener's becoming accustomed to fixing himself in the center of his "quad" room in order to reap the full benefits of stunning, three-dimensional sound.

Will the average record fan accept the high cost and the static seating arrangement? The jury is still out on these questions. If quadrasonic sound follows the patterns of the hi-fi and stereo crazes, it will most certainly be for the masses; and people will soon be referring to their playback systems as "quads" rather than "stereos." But if the quad system fails to find a home in the average living room it may end up in the automobile. The playback components would be smaller in a car, and therefore far less costly, and, of course, people are accustomed to sitting in fixed positions as they drive.

What will be the next great technical advance in recorded sound after quad? The only thing to be certain of is change itself. Most likely, the disc in one form or another will remain with us for years to come. Although this history is confined to sound, it is interesting, parenthetically, to note that Teldec, a German electronics firm in partnership with British Decca, has already developed a workable high-speed plastic disc (1,800 rpm) able to reproduce pictures and sound simultaneously. Both Philips, the giant electronics firm based in the Netherlands, and the Musical Corporation of America (MCA) have independently announced similar breakthroughs. Naturally, the audio-visual disc will require special playback equipment; and neither the machine nor the disc has been marketed commercially as of this writing. But the advent of the video disc does highlight the almost limitless potential of disc recording.

Although the disc has proven in the past to be tough, resilient and adaptable, it, too, may become obsolete. In fact, one day we may dispense completely with the practice of buying our recorded entertainment on either records or tape. In the future, our houses and apartments may be linked by cable to vast tape libraries that will offer a tremendous variety of all forms of recorded entertainment, performed by the popular artists of the day. Such systems are already in use on a small scale in a number of educational institutions. By dialing a series of numbers over a telephone wire to a computer, a teacher may have a specific recording transmitted directly to her classroom. Larger, more sophisticated services may one day be offered to us by cable television companies, which are already busily wiring the world. Theoretically, the cable television operator would charge a nominal fee for each recording piped into a home, varying with its length or description. The computer could be programmed to record the number of times that each recording in the library was played in a given period of time, and to calculate the shares of the fees collected to go to the recording artist, the record company and the publisher of the music.

All of this is hypothetical, of course. And perhaps the manner in which recorded entertainment is conveyed to the public in the future is not of paramount importance. What matters is that millions of people will continue to pay to hear the music that they want to hear *when* they want to hear it. For as long as that willingness persists, there will be a recording industry.

PART TWO

The Anatomy of a Record Company

19

Breaking into the Field

Today there are hundreds of record companies located in the United States, and hundreds more abroad. The American market absorbs a little less than one-half the total number of records and prerecorded tapes produced throughout the world, not including the output of the state-run record labels in the Communist Bloc countries.

Record companies range in size from extremely small operations that are little more than hobbies for the people that run them, to giant international combines with far-flung satellite and subsidiary operations. CBS/Columbia, E.M.I./Capitol, British Decca–London, Philips/Mercury/DGG and RCA Victor are among the giants. There are also conglomerates (collections of record labels under one ownership) that rival and sometimes surpass the internationally based combines. The Kinney Group is an outstanding example. Today, the combined sales of this conglomerate (Warner Brothers, Reprise, Elektra, Nonesuch, Atlantic and Atco) make it the number-one record organization in the United States.

The Anatomy of a Record Company

The combines and the conglomerates, each employing thousands, dominate the record industry in the western world, and in several Oriental countries. The power, prestige and strong bargaining capabilities of these organizations is an established fact; yet their presence on the scene has not discouraged new labels from entering the highly competitive record market every year.

Why do so many entrepreneurs invest in the record trade in the face of such competition and long odds? The answer is that the risks involved appear to be worthwhile. The record business is an important and glamorous part of the entertainment world. It has a strong romantic allure not only because records are popular and fun to listen to, but also because the record trade is one in which rags-to-riches stories are not uncommon. Besides, at first glance, the financial requirements for entering the business seem modest in relation to the potential rewards. The capital investment needed can be relatively small.

A small record company does not have to own a recording studio; it can rent one when necessary. Record pressing plants and tape duplicating facilities in various parts of the country can be used by anyone who can afford them; even factories operated by the major record companies are open for use by the small record firm. However, pressing costs are a relatively minor concern for the small operator. The most important factor, or the "big nut" as they say, is the cost of talent and studio production.

A long-playing record of a guitar-strumming folk singer can cost as little as fifteen hundred dollars, including payment to the artist at union scale, and studio rental charges. However, costs escalate rapidly with the addition of studio musicians, singers, arrangers and copyists.

174

In fact, studio musician rates paid in America are by far the highest in the world. A side musician at a recording session in New York earns about three times as much as his British counterpart at a recording session in London. This is why American record companies have severely curtailed programs to record large-scale works, particularly symphonic works, in the United States. For example, a recording by Leonard Bernstein and the New York Philharmonic of Beethoven's Symphony No. 3 ("Eroica") would require, under American Federation of Musicians rules, at least three recording sessions lasting three hours each. This could cost as much as thirty thousand dollars for musicians' salaries alone. Yet the sales potential of the recording would be only a fraction of that of a new release by Blood, Sweat and Tears, a group made up of a very few musicians. As a result, today most large-scale recording projects take place in Europe. The few companies that continue to record symphony orchestras in the United States do so for prestige. Needless to say, only the very largest and most prosperous can afford to pay the exorbitant costs. Therefore, all new labels planning to record in the United States must, out of economic necessity, confine themselves to pop music. But even in this field the going is far from easy.

Nevertheless, several record companies originally started on shoestrings have been enormously successful. A case in point is the incredible story of Herb Alpert and A&M Records. Some years ago, Alpert attempted to persuade a number of leading record labels to record his Tijuana Brass group — each time in vain. As a last resort, he scraped together enough money to record the band himself. The outcome is a legend. The Tijuana Brass turned out a steady stream of hit singles and albums. But Alpert was not content to rest on his laurels: he assembled a staff of skilled producers and promotional people who were able to seek out new talent and anticipate new trends in the public's taste, with fortunate results. A&M Records is now a multimillion dollar operation with a history of consistent success. When the Tijuana Brass faded in popularity, A&M found the Carpenters, who have more than filled the void. And it is a good bet that Alpert and his staff will continue to find new recording talent to sustain their success.

The modern record industry has yielded other impressive success stories. The brilliant Barry Gordie turned Detroit into the soul music capital of the world by means of his extensive Tamala-Motown organization. He, too, started in the business with virtually no capital. So did Ahmet Ertigan and Jerry Wexler, the founders of the Atlantic-Atco empire, and Jack Holtzman, who started Elektra Records on a bet.

But the truth of the matter is that the Alperts, the Gordies, Ertigans, and Wexlers, when compared to the hundreds of others who have attempted to make their fortunes in records, are extremely rare. The investment may be low in comparison to making refrigerators or motorcycles, but a newcomer's chances of striking it rich in records are slim.

The competition arrayed against a fledgling popular record label is overwhelming. Literally thousands of new singles and long-playing records flood the market every year in a seemingly endless stream. All of the new records vie for the limited space available on dealers' shelves. Even the radio industry, which relies so heavily on records for program material, is incapable of coping with the flood. According to a survey taken a few years ago, only 30 percent of all of the pop singles released in the United States are ever broadcast. Albums fare somewhat better. The same survey indicated that about 60 percent of new long-play releases are heard on the air at one time or another. These are particularly telling statistics. Since it is a rule of thumb that musical records do not sell without radio play, 70 percent of all pop single releases and 40 percent of all long plays are automatically doomed to fail at the moment they are released because there is not enough broadcast capacity to promote them.

To better understand the odds of succeeding in today's recording industry, suppose our new record company is fortunate enough to produce one or two records that appeal to radio stations and are given some air play. Let's assume that the air exposure generates orders for the records. Now our company is faced with a fresh set of problems: selling records and collecting bills. The record distribution problems of the small firm are formidable. To be successful, a company must be in a position to exert enough power to get decent sales representation in the face of competition from hundreds of other labels, and, most important, to collect money due from the sale of records. The major firms control their own distributional networks, either through wholly owned sales branches and retail stores, or through distributors who agree to sell their records to the exclusion of most other labels.

The medium-sized or small label must resort to a none too reliable network of independent record distributors, of which there are usually several in each large city.

These so-called independent wholesalers invariably represent one or more medium-sized labels: A&M, Paramount, Bell, and Mercury, for example, plus as many as fifty or more smaller labels. In this arena, the small operator must fight to win the attention and support of the distributors' sales and promotional people.

The independent distributor, then, is a key man, and often a harried man to deal with. He is faced with the problem of collecting bills from retailers and rack jobbers. Those distributors whose businesses have survived over the years have found it difficult to be loyal to any record label, large or small, since most record companies have a habit of switching from one distributor to another at the slightest provocation.

In short, the record market is a jungle where only the hardiest and most resourceful labels can survive.

A number of the smaller record firms blessed with success have found it more efficient to concentrate on producing hits than on selling them. These labels will lease their recordings to larger firms, or make distribution pacts with the major labels. Not a few successful medium-sized companies have been willing to sell out lock, stock and barrel to larger companies.

But in spite of the rather gloomy prospects facing any new record company, it is safe to assume that new labels bent on emulating the histories of Motown, Atlantic, A&M and Elektra will continue to sprout up in sizable numbers. For as long as it still is possible, with the necessary talent and knowledgeability, to snatch the brass ring, the small record firm will continue to emerge.

20

The Structure

THERE ARE, of course, other ways to embark on a career in the record business without having to start one's own company. As most such opportunities exist within the larger firms, we will now examine the typical structure of a major American record company, bearing in mind that a small company must perform the same basic functions with far fewer people.

A modern record company invariably consists of a major label and a cluster of smaller labels, each of which is designed to serve a special market. In addition, the major record company usually distributes several independent record labels. For example, the CBS/Columbia group owns and distributes a bread-and-butter label, Columbia, as well as Epic Records (a pop label), Harmony Records (a low-priced long-play line), Odyssey Records (a medium-priced classical line of mainly older recordings) and Okeh Records (specializing in jazz and soul recordings). Among the outside labels it distributes are Monument Records, Barnaby Records and Stax/Volt.

Although no two major companies are operated exactly in the same manner, the following activities are fairly standard throughout the industry.

Administration

The head of a company, and of course its chief administrator, is the president. All operating divisional and department heads report to him either directly, or indirectly, usually through the office of the executive vice-president, who is charged with carrying out the president's policies and who operates the company from day to day.

The president is left free to make major decisions and to determine the future direction of the company in light of current trends. He is invariably involved in high-level negotiations for the rights to Broadway and Hollywood show albums and major artist contracts. Another important part of his job is maintaining relationships with the company's top recording stars and their agents.

Perhaps his most important function is to act as the final arbiter between those of his staff who create the recorded product (artists and repertoire) and those who sell it (the marketing department). It is traditional in the record business that the two factions rarely agree.

In addition, the president is also responsible for overseeing the activities of several specialized administrative staffs. These are:

The Business Affairs Department

The business affairs staff is responsible for all business arrangements with artists, publishers, unions and outside producers. As one might expect, the personnel of the department is generally made up of lawyers and accountants, with the usual complement of secretaries and file clerks.

The Legal Department

The legal department drafts and/or approves all contracts and licenses the company negotiates with artists, publishers, labor unions and suppliers. The legal staff is also charged with the responsibility of keeping ahead of contract renewals. There have been occasions when the legal department of a record company has allowed an artist's contract to lapse, and then has had to renegotiate the agreement at a much stiffer price.

As the record industry has grown in complexity, the role of the lawyer has increased in importance. It is not uncommon today to find lawyers in many key managerial positions throughout the industry.

The Accounting Department

The accounting department is the domain of the financial vice-president, or controller, whichever the company chooses to call him. His responsibilities are truly awesome, and in a large company he relies on a corps of assistant controllers to see that they are successfully carried out. These assistants operate in two general areas: accounts payable and accounts receivable.

The accounts payable wing of the department is, as its name implies, responsible for making all of the company's disbursements: advance payments to artists, artist royalties, copyright fees to music publishers, employees' paychecks, and payments due to outside companies that supply the record company with materials and services. Disbursement of artist royalties and copyright fees alone is an enormous undertaking for a company selling millions of recordings each year.

The accounts receivable section bills and collects for the records the company sells. A large record company may sell to as many as eight thousand different retail outlets in the United States alone. It may have hundreds of customers abroad, and it may manufacture records and tapes for many smaller firms. Preparing accurate invoices for so many accounts, and keeping tabs on the collection of bills, requires a host of highly qualified specialists, including first-rate accountants, bookkeepers, credit managers and clerks.

In view of the tremendous work load that an accounting staff in a record firm must bear, it is not surprising that the recording industry was one of the first to make use of the services of the computer.

Data Processing

The computer establishment in a large record company, particularly one that operates a record club, is an extremely important department. Its function is to store vast quantities of information for use in paying artist royalties and publisher copyright fees, maintaining inventory controls, invoicing customers, recording sales statistics, and handling the payroll. The department consists of a relatively large staff of computer specialists: systems and procedures experts, programmers, and keypunch operators.

So much for the president's immediate staff. Here now are the other divisions that report to him:

The Operations Division

The operations division consists of a group of employees with a wide range of skills and specialties, mostly of a technical nature. The division is traditionally involved in all phases of record production: studio operations, record manufacturing, tape duplication, and warehousing and purchasing.

Studio Operations

The large company normally operates three or four studio installations in the United States, usually located in the nation's three principal recording centers — New York, Los Angeles and Nashville. Each installation includes one to five studios of varying sizes. Each studio is equipped with a control room, complete with mixing boards, or consoles, and tape recorders. These facilities are primarily for the use of the company's own A&R staff, but quite often they are made available to smaller record companies on a rental basis.

Record Plants

Most major record companies operate two to four record pressing and prerecorded tape duplicating plants in the United States. These are situated in localities best suited to serve high-density population areas.

The pressing plant is a complex operation. It houses an electroplating department that produces the metal stampers from which records are pressed, the record presses themselves, and warehousing and shipping facilities. Most of the large companies have added high-speed tape-duplicating facilities that turn out thousands of eight-track, four-track and cassette cartridges.

The trained personnel needed to operate a modern record and tape manufacturing installation are extremely varied. They run the gamut from highly skilled professionals to semiskilled and unskilled labor. Because of the importance of the electroplating operation and the mixing of the organic chemical compounds used in the record pressings, one or more chemical engineers are invariably on the staff. There are also press operators, tape duplicator operators, production expediters, order service

A modern record pressing and tape duplicating facility:
the RCA Victor plant at Indianapolis, Indiana

clerks who coordinate production with sales, warehouse-men, shipping clerks, traffic specialists and a host of less specialized employees.

The Purchasing Department

A major company's purchases of electronic equipment, office supplies, chemicals, blank tapes, record jackets, tape cases and containers, printed album covers and other materials involve the expenditure of millions of dollars a year. Since the company calculates its average profit from each record to the penny, it is extremely important that it employ knowledgeable, proficient purchasing agents who are capable of buying high-grade equipment and materials at the best possible prices.

184

The Inventory Control Department

The inventory control department is made up of specialists who determine the number of records and tapes to be manufactured. They base their calculations upon current and past sales statistics, and in anticipation of the company's future inventory requirements. This is a very delicate responsibility in a company carrying thousands of titles in its catalogue. If too many records are produced, the warehouse shelves will be loaded with records that will take months and even years to sell, or that might even have to be ultimately scrapped. If too few records are produced, the company will lose sales. Mistakes made in either direction are costly.

The Research and Development Department

Only the largest record companies can afford the luxury of a research and development department. The research staff is made up of electronic engineers and technicians, and chemical engineers. Their collective task is to improve the general quality of recorded sound reproduction, record pressings and tape duplicates. If the research staff hits upon a revolutionary technical advance and the company is able to steal a march on its competitors, so much the better. Columbia's development of the long-playing record and the new Teldec audio-visual disc are two examples that come to mind readily. But more often, the achievements of the researchers are more modest and are rarely brought to the attention of the public. Added together, however, these achievements are responsible for the superior quality of recordings today.

The Marketing Division

The selling, or marketing, organization is one of a company's most important divisions. It takes charge of a recording from the time the A&R staff schedules it for release to the time of its purchase by a record fan.

The first step in this process is to provocatively and attractively package the album or tape so that it will appeal to customers when displayed in record stores and store windows. The second step is to make the public aware of the recording through publicity: air play and advertising. The third step, of course, is to sell it to record retail outlets.

A record marketing staff is comprised of a variety of professionals and specialists, all reporting directly or indirectly to the head of the division: a national sales manager, regional sales managers, promotion managers, product managers, sales branch managers, salesmen, advertising specialists, publicity specialists, graphic artists, writers, proofreaders, and radio and television promotion specialists.

The International Division

The international activities of a major record company are twofold: to sell and promote the records of American artists abroad, and to seek out foreign artists who may have sales potential in the United States. Most of the major record complexes are either American-based, owning subsidiary companies scattered around the globe; or they are European operations with extensive representation in the United States. CBS/Columbia and RCA Victor are the most notable examples of the American-owned international combine. Mercury, Capitol and London are all currently owned by European interests. In fact, for the past two decades many of the top-selling records on American best-seller charts have originated in foreign studios.

The Artist and Repertoire Division

The artists and repertoire division is, of course, the hub of any record company. If a record label cannot consistently offer the kinds of records that the public will buy, it will soon find itself in deep trouble, no matter how efficiently and skillfully it is managed in all its other divisions.

The A&R division in a large firm is divided into two departments: classical recordings and popular recordings. Since the sale of classical recordings in the United States amounts to only about 7 or 8 percent of the total number of records sold, it stands to reason that the popular staff far outnumbers the classical staff. Furthermore, members of the popular staff are based in the three key entertainment centers for recordings — New York, Los Angeles and Nashville — while a classical A&R staff is confined to one city — traditionally New York.

Each A&R man, working within his particular sphere, whether it be classical, popular, soul, country and western, folk, jazz or rock, has two basic responsibilities: he must record to the best advantage an assigned group of artists under contract to the company; and he must be on the alert for potential new talent for the label.

Artist and repertoire jobs are the most eagerly sought after in the record industry — and the most difficult to land. Not only are they the most glamorous jobs, they are among the highest paying in the business. And this is as it should be, because a record company's success depends heavily on the quality and appeal of its recordings. In a small company, a successful producer can virtually write his own ticket. The major labels reward hit-making producers with generous bonuses.

Most of the current generation of successful pop A&R men are comparatively young and have a "feel" for what will sell in a youth-oriented record market. Unfortunately, record history has proven that as an A&R man achieves experience and prestige, it is usually at the expense of his continuing ability to anticipate new trends in the public's musical taste and to adapt to them. All too often, the highly successful pop producer is deluded into thinking that he is actually setting the standards for popular music. In fact, public taste is fickle and subject to immediate and sudden change; often even the greatest producers are left far behind the new trends, still clinging to their old habits and standards. Age also has a lot to do with an A&R man's success or failure. It is probably safe to say that as most A&R men grow older they gradually lose their ability to hear the elements in popular music that turn teen-agers on. For this reason the average career of a pop record producer is relatively short.

Becoming an A&R man is not simple. Many producers gain their experience and win their credentials by producing recordings with groups and artists not yet signed to a label, with the hope of selling the record masters to an established company. Often, these aspiring producers make their own financial investments in the sessions. A promising master recording can be the object of very spirited bidding among record firms in search of a hit. But should no interest be shown, the producer must sustain the loss himself.

A few highly successful producers have found their way into recording studios by way of reporting and editorial jobs on record trade magazines. Their obvious ability to grasp market conditions and to forecast future trends in music so impressed high-level record executives that they were hired to make recordings.

A less spectacular way to become an A&R man is to qualify as a trainee-producer in one of the major record firms. Unfortunately, trainee programs are not always available, particularly during times when business conditions are bad. Even when such programs are in effect, few candidates who apply are chosen. Those who are must be exceptional. A college degree and a proven ability to read music and play an instrument is almost mandatory. Today, if a candidate can write music and can orchestrate, he will be looked upon with particular favor. (It is ironic that the personnel managers at the major companies continue to look for these last credentials when it is an established fact that some of the greatest A&R men of all times cannot distinguish one musical note from another.)

No matter what entrée the A&R man has had to the business, his real training occurs in the recording studio. There, by observing and assisting an established producer, whether independent or on the staff of a record company, he learns the capabilities of recording equipment, the names of performing union contractors who deliver the best side musicians and chorus singers, and how to extract the best possible performance from the recording artist or group. These skills must be mastered quickly, since competition for the few A&R jobs available at any time is very keen. But the experience of organizing and directing recording sessions stands the new A&R man in good stead for the future. Many top A&R men go on to top executive positions in the industry and in other fields of entertainment.

21
How the Seed Is Sown

ONE of the most fascinating aspects of the record business is the "chemistry" that takes place during the creation of a recording. How, for instance, were artists like the Carpenters, Elton John, Simon and Garfunkel, Andy Williams, Barbra Streisand, Tom Jones or Bob Dylan discovered and signed to recording contracts? How are the "right" songs or material chosen? What part does the A&R man play; and how important is he to the commercial success of a recording?

As the record business has grown, the A&R function has become more complex and more vital. But the three basic ingredients of a great recording — an artist who can communicate with a great many people, an outstanding song or piece of music, and the treatment given the musical material — have remained unchanged since the great days of the Gaisberg brothers in the Gay Nineties.

The simplest but by far the most expensive way for a record company to acquire top-drawer talent is simply to buy it. Established recording stars or artists on the rise who are free of contract obligations are a scarce commodity. However, occasionally a top star in search of greener fields will negotiate with competing labels as the expiration date of his recording contract approaches. It also is not uncommon for small labels to free young stars of their recording contract obligations in consideration of cash payments. Whenever either situation occurs, and if a star or a potential star is at stake, high-powered negotiations and fierce competitive bidding are certain to follow.

Early in the 1950s, when Elvis Presley was a young regular on the Louisiana Hayride radio show originating in Shreveport, a record of his on the Sun label began to look as if it might be a hit. The title of the record was "That's All Right." As it began to scale the best-seller charts, Presley's business manager, Colonel Tom Parker, began negotiating new recording agreements with several large record firms, apparently confident that he would be able to free Elvis from his commitments to the then-struggling Sun label. And he was right. Sun was unable to resist the thirty-five thousand dollars proffered by Colonel Parker, and soon thereafter Elvis was making records for RCA Victor. With the new-found cash, Sun was able to promote another recording artist to stardom with yet another smash hit single, the first million seller in the label's history. The artist was Johnny Cash and the song was "I Walk the Line." This time Columbia bought the recording and Cash's contract with Sun for a substantial sum.

Over a decade ago, another sure-fire young singing star by the name of Andy Williams found himself in the unusual position of being free to negotiate for his future recording services. At the time, Williams was the chief asset of the Cadence record label, which was owned by Archie Bleyer, the former music director of the Arthur Godfrey radio show. Bleyer executed one of the greatest coups in modern record history. He issued a long-playing record called "The First Family," a satire of President Kennedy and his family. The recording was phenomenally successful. Millions of copies were sold within the span of a few months. Bleyer apparently decided that nothing he would ever do in the future could match that success, so he shut the Cadence operation down. Andy Williams wisely bought the rights to his Cadence masters and signed a long-term contract with Columbia Records.

There are more recent examples of major artists switching labels. The Philadelphia Orchestra, perhaps the most popular symphonic organization in the world, left Columbia after decades for RCA Victor, reportedly for fatter guarantees. The Rolling Stones, for years a top-selling act on the London label, signed a contract with the American-based Atlantic label for an unreported, but undoubtedly considerable, amount of money and guarantees. Johnny Winter, the albino singing sensation, enjoyed a hit album or two on the Imperial label, and then received guarantees for hundreds of thousands of dollars as a reward for signing a contract with Columbia.

A less expensive way for record companies to obtain artists of stellar rank is to acquire rights to recordings by foreign stars through licensing agreements with subsidiary or affiliated companies located abroad. For several years the Beatles' recordings were produced by E.M.I., the parent company of Capitol Records. Capitol literally rode the wave of Beatlemania on the coattails of its British affiliate. Ironically, the group that became the Beatles' closest competitor, the Dave Clark Five, was also under contract to E.M.I., and thus technically available to Capitol. But Capitol decided not to issue Dave Clark Five recordings, probably because the group's style was so similar to the Beatles'. The group's recordings were ultimately licensed to Epic Records, a wholly owned subsidiary of CBS/Columbia, one of Capitol's arch-rivals in the United States.

A high proportion of recordings by foreign artists, particularly British artists, have scored very well on the bestseller charts in the last ten years. Tom Jones, the Who, Petula Clark, Lulu, and Joe Cocker are only a few such artists that immediately come to mind.

The great attraction of licensing foreign recordings is that the purchaser of the license bears none of the recording expenses. Aside from promotional and manufacturing costs, an American firm merely pays pressing fees, artist royalties and copyright fees as copies of a foreign recording are sold. However, licensing arrangements between American and European firms are almost always reciprocal. In other words, an American label seeking top European talent must be in a position to offer top American talent in exchange.

Another way for recording companies to acquire top talent, if only for one album, is to obtain the rights to record a Broadway musical. However, this is not a league for the petty spender or the faint of heart. It is fairly easy for many of us to recall the names of some of the great hit productions of the last thirty years, among them *Hair, Oh, Calcutta!, Fiddler on the Roof, My Fair Lady,*

Camelot, West Side Story, South Pacific and *Hello, Dolly!;*
but only a handful of dedicated students of the American
musical theater will remember any of the hundreds of
shows, many of them recorded, that failed and were
consigned to oblivion.

The cost of staging a Broadway musical is exorbitant,
and for many years Broadway producers found the recording industry a prime source of ready and often substantial
cash. Columbia's incredible success with *My Fair Lady*
in 1956 set the pattern. Goddard Lieberson, then Columbia's executive vice-president and chief A&R man, persuaded the CBS hierarchy to invest heavily in the show
during its formative stages. In fact, CBS wound up the
biggest angel; but the huge corporation was repaid many,
many times over. Lieberson's reward was the presidency
of the CBS Records division.

For several years following, Lieberson continued to display a golden touch. He personally produced a string of
highly successful Broadway musical albums including
Camelot, West Side Story and *The Sound of Music*, which
further enriched the CBS coffers. Naturally, Columbia's
rivals were very anxious to emulate Lieberson's success
and thus share in the Broadway bonanza. Musical producers found themselves in a veritable dream world where
recording company executives fought for the privilege of
investing hundreds of thousands of dollars in show properties that were often of dubious merit. Even Lieberson, a
thoroughly sophisticated and urbane man with many years'
experience on the Broadway scene, was caught up in the
madness. The outcome was predictable. A good portion
of the profits CBS had reaped from *My Fair Lady* was
dissipated on forgettable shows like *All American, Kean,*

Bravo, Giovanni, Subways Are for Sleeping and *We Take the Town.* When the dust finally settled, the scorecard indicated that CBS had bankrolled eight major flops in a row.

This unsettling experience, together with similar if less disastrous developments at other companies, led industry leaders to approach the musical stage more soberly by the end of 1963. To be sure, Broadway has produced its complement of hits since that time, but very few have made a notable impression in record shops. Today record companies do, of course, continue to record Broadway musicals, but they are very carefully selected. If a company makes a financial contribution to a production, it is usually modest.

Recording companies are almost invariably willing to allow their artists under contract to record show albums for competing labels. This tolerance dates from a lesson learned the hard way in the industry.

Some years ago, Decca Records refused to permit Ethel Merman to re-create for records her stage triumph *Call Me Madam* with members of the original cast. This happened after RCA Victor had secured recording rights to the show. Red-faced Victor executives were forced to record the show with Dinah Shore substituting in the leading role. Later Miss Merman recorded her role in the show with a pickup cast on Decca. Since the stage production had been from its inception tailored to Miss Merman's talents, it should not be too difficult to guess which of the two albums sold better. Needless to say, a recording company negotiating for the rights to record a show today makes doubly sure that all cast members have been cleared for recording *before* the contract is signed.

The Anatomy of a Record Company

Hollywood continues to be a valuable source of hit album material for the old-line record labels, but only rarely. Motion picture companies have invaded the record industry in recent years. Virtually every major Hollywood studio owns or is associated with a record label. Naturally, any promising movie sound track is assigned to the film company's recording affiliate. The sound track album of *Love Story* infused new life into the ailing Paramount Records organization. The sound track from MGM's production of *2001* kept the foundering record arm of the famous film company in business for an additional year or two. But, actually, few of the movie industry's ventures in recording have proved highly successful. MGM recently sold its interests in the record industry, perhaps setting a reverse trend for Hollywood.

In an affluent recording company, a large, ready cash reserve is set aside for the acquisition of promising talent, particularly groups. The enterprising independent producer who can forge new groups from gifted but unattached rock musicians capable of producing "commercial" music will find that he is in a seller's market with much-sought-after properties.

The independent producer usually receives a share of the revenues earned by the group, including artist royalties. To protect itself, the recording company will stipulate that the group has to remain with the label when and if the group and its producer decide to sever their relationship. James William Guercio, the mentor of the group Chicago, is one of the most successful independent producers in the game. Although Chicago is under an exclusive contract to Columbia, Guercio nevertheless maintains complete artistic control over all phases of the group's recording activities.

There are a number of successful independent producers besides Guercio. Don Kirschner has often displayed the Midas touch. He personally recruited the members of the Monkees, a group that starred in a Beatles-inspired television situation comedy for several years and recorded several hit albums and singles. Kirschner also formed a group for the sound track of the Harlem Globetrotters cartoon TV series.

Many prominent artists and producers prefer to operate under an independent label, leaving the time-consuming and expensive business of distribution of their recordings to a larger company. This allows them the freedom to concentrate on more creative matters — at a price, of course. The Beatles' Apple Records (distributed by Capitol) is one example that immediately comes to mind. Of course, there are many others. The drawback to the distribution arrangement is that the distributing company may tend to give preferential treatment to its own recordings, sometimes at the expense of the smaller label's inventory.

A company's acquisition of talent through independent producers has become commonplace. But the most economical, and by far the most preferable, way for a company to find talent is to develop its own. This still happens. Simon and Garfunkel, Bob Dylan, and Glenn Campbell were discovered by A&R men at CBS and Capitol. Barbra Streisand was signed to a contract at the insistence of a group of Columbia salesmen who had seen her perform in a featured role in a short-lived Broadway musical called *I Can Get It For You Wholesale.*

A&R men must constantly stay abreast of new acts and artists appearing on the night-club circuit or at rock festivals; and many still continue to listen to demonstration records and tapes submitted to the company to be auditioned. Every major recording company in pop music is literally deluged with hundreds of these "demos" every year. An astute producer with a good ear for contemporary pop music can usually determine right away whether the artist or group he is auditioning has commercial potential. Of course, there have been instances of A&R men failing to hear the commercial potential of artists or material submitted to them. E.M.I. turned down the Who's recording of *Tommy*, for example.

Unfortunately, a number of leading recording firms have recently adopted a policy of returning all demos received from unknown sources without listening to them. This is a protective measure. Too often owners of rejected demos have claimed that their submitted material has been stolen by a firm or its artists, and they have filed suit for damages. Many of the companies that have been plagued by this practice now will not permit their A&R staffs to listen to a demo unless the owner can prove that the offered material has been published and copyrighted.

The bitter truth is that the vast majority of demos, even those that are heard by A&R men, are consigned to the wastepaper basket. But the exercise proves worthwhile when a group of the quality of the Band, Guess Who, or Emerson, Lake and Palmer is discovered and launched as new recording stars.

22

Paying the Artist

ONCE the A&R staff of a recording company becomes convinced that an artist or a group has the potential to make recordings that will sell, the artist is asked to sign a contract. The terms of a recording agreement are fairly standard throughout the industry. They will invariably stipulate that the artist must record for the company exclusively for a specified length of time, usually for one year. Beyond that date, the company reserves the right to extend the term of the contract for additional one-year periods, up to three or four. In short, the company can tie up the artist for four or five years at its own election. Should the company decide not to exercise its option at the end of any one-year period, the terms of the contract will nevertheless prohibit the artist from rerecording the selections he or she has made for the company for a competing label. This restriction remains in effect for a five-year period, commencing on the date each selection was recorded. This provision protects the recording company from having its former artists duplicate their best material for rival firms.

The contract will also state that the company guarantees to produce a minimum number of recordings with the artist in each one-year period. If the artist is a singer, the American Federation of Television and Radio Artists (AFTRA) is responsible for setting his or her minimum wage. Recording minimums for musicians is the province of the American Federation of Musicians (AFM). Under the terms of the agreements between the recording companies and the performing unions, all artists employed by the companies are required to be dues-paying members of either AFTRA or AFM. But the unions do not arrange specific rates for individual artists; each artist is free to negotiate for as much as he or she can command.

A typical recording contract further states that initial payments made to the artist are to be considered advances charged against the artist's future royalty earnings. All of the creative costs incurred at recording sessions, including the salaries of side musicians, singers, arrangers and music copyists, and instrument cartage fees, are also charged against the artist's royalties. A number of companies also apply sound-engineering expenses to the artist's account. Since an unproven artist is seldom granted a royalty rate of more than 2 or 3 percent of the retail list price of his or her recording, the recording must be very successful if these advances and charges are to be recouped, and if the artist is to make any money at all.

As if to make the plight of the young recording artist even more difficult, advances, fees, and expenses charged against the artist's royalties are accumulated, or pooled. For example, the company may release five of the artist's recordings without obtaining any appreciable retail sales reaction. If the artist's sixth release becomes a hit, his or her royalty earnings from that recording will be used to repay the costs of *all six recordings*.

On the surface it would appear that the company is taking unfair advantage of the artist. However, it must be remembered that for each recording the company assumes many expenses of its own, including the cost of advertising and promotion, payments to music copyright proprietors, operating and manufacturing overhead and so on. Losses incurred in the production of recordings that never sell very well are also necessarily absorbed by the company. And since very few recordings released in this country appear on the best-seller charts, the advance accounts ledger in the average recording firm usually shows a good amount of red ink.

To understand more accurately how the system works, let's take the hypothetical case of a singer, who, during three recording sessions, records twelve songs at a cost of nine thousand dollars. His recording company decides to release two of the songs on a pop single record. The company arranges to pay the artist royalties based on 90 percent, rather than 100 percent, of the total number of records that will be sold, claiming justifiably that it needs the 10 percent deduction to cover the cost of future returns of defective or shopworn records. The singer's contract stipulates that he be paid a royalty rate of 3 percent. Therefore, on a pop single that sells for $1.00, the company pays the artist 3 percent of 90 percent of $1.00 for each copy of the record it sells. This amounts to 2.7¢ per record. Let's say it turns out that the single successfully sells 500,000 copies. Our singer's gross royalty earnings are:

$$500{,}000 \text{ x } 2.7\text{¢} = \$13{,}500.$$

However, the recording company still must deduct the total cost of the artist's three recording sessions, nine thousand dollars. Thus, our singer will receive forty-five hundred dollars when the company distributes its next batch of royalty checks, usually done once every six months.

But there is more to come. Since the artist's single has been so successful, the company decides to release the recording in the long-play album format, using ten other selections recorded during the original three sessions to round out the record. The company pegs the retail selling price of the album at $4.98. However, the company decides to make further deductions before establishing our singer's royalty base. There is, of course, the standard 10 percent deduction for returns, as in the case of the pop single record; but also deducted is the cost of printing and fabricating the record jacket. The company's justification for this deduction is that the artist is not entitled to derive income from the sale of any component of an album other than the disc itself. In most cases, the deduction for album packaging averages about 12 percent, or 60¢ on a $4.98 album, thus reducing the artist's royalty base to $4.38. To sum up, the artist is paid according to the following formula:

Suggested retail list price	$4.98
Less packaging cost (12%)	—.60
	4.38
Less return allowance (10%)	—.44
	3.94
Artist's royalty rate (3%)	×.03
Artist's earnings per album	.1182

Assuming that the company sells fifty thousand albums, the artist will earn $5,910. At this point the company need make no deductions for recording session expenses since these were paid off by the artist's single-record royalties. So our singer has netted a total of $10,410 from the combined sales of the single record and the album, and this amount is an exceptional achievement for a new artist. Should the company decide later to release the artist's recorded material in tape cartridges, the artist will derive more income.

It is not at all uncommon for a recording company to increase the royalty rate in a contract with a young artist after he or she has achieved stardom. The increase usually brings the rate up to a 5 or 6 percent royalty, though recently royalties for top recording acts have zoomed to 15 percent or more. On occasion a company will actually guarantee an artist a specified annual income from royalties. Artists who win these contract terms are paid whether their recordings sell or not. Naturally, only the most prominent recording stars with histories of consistent success are awarded such terms. Even so, a guaranteed royalty agreement can backfire, with a company continuing to pay substantial amounts of money to a former star whose recordings no longer sell at all.

As we have seen, only the superstars of the recording world amass fortunes from recording royalties. Night clubs, motion pictures and television are generally more lucrative; so are rock concerts and festivals. However, most entertainers and their managers know the enormous boost a smash hit album or single can give them in the other media. As a promotional tool, recording can be essential to the career of an entertainer.

The Anatomy of a Record Company

The rewards in store for the star who can write hit songs as well as perform them are very great, indeed. John Lennon, Paul McCartney, Paul Simon, Bob Dylan and Burt Bacharach have, to be sure, earned tidy sums in recording royalties; but far greater is the income these artists earn on their music copyrights.

The term copyright simply means the right to copy. Once a writer registers a musical composition with the Copyright Office of the United States government, only the writer has the right to make copies of the work for free, either in print or in recordings. Anyone else wanting to use the composition must obtain the permission of the writer, which is granted under a license, and for a fee. When copyrighting, the writer may stipulate his right to arrange for the first recording of his composition. However, once the initial recording has been made and becomes available to the public, the writer may not prevent others from making their own recorded versions of his composition, provided that the performances are in good taste and that the copyright fee is paid to the writer. This fee is established by federal law. In popular music, it is two cents for each record and tape copy sold. The rate for symphonic or extended musical works is two cents for the first eight minutes of music, and one-quarter of a cent for each minute of playing time thereafter.

A songwriter almost always assigns a publisher to manage his copyright. In return, the publisher is expected to present the writer's composition to recording companies, to produce demonstration records and tapes, to manage film and television rights, and to collect fees. A reputable, enterprising publisher is an invaluable asset to the modern songwriter.

Paying the Artist

The standard business arrangement between writer and publisher is to share equally all revenues derived from the writer's copyrights. If, for example, a recording yields 500,000 pop single sales, the copyright fees (at the rate of 2¢ per record sold) would amount to a total of $10,000. Publisher and writer then net $5,000 each. But the potential income from a hit song does not end here.

The publisher usually will try to persuade other recording stars and recording companies to make additional recorded versions of the hit song. These are called "covers" in the trade. It is not at all unusual for a hit tune to be "covered" fifty or sixty times, most often in the album format. To persuade even more companies to make "covers," the publisher will often grant copyright licenses at lower rates than the standard 2¢ per record. An enterprising music publisher will also have publishing contacts abroad. The standard business arrangement between American and foreign publishers is that they share equally the income derived from the American house's compositions in the foreign country. Since the songwriter must in turn divide all of the income earned from his copyrights with his publisher, it follows that he will receive 25 percent of the foreign revenues.

Only rarely will a tune falling short of the hit charts be sold in sheet music. But the songwriter lucky enough to see his song in print can expect a reasonably good income from it, about fifteen cents for each copy of sheet music sold. With the current trend to books and folio editions of popular music anthologies, and stage and marching band arrangements of contemporary hits, the print music market will become increasingly lucrative for the successful songwriter. So will the booming foreign sheet music market, though it yields only about half the royalty rate he receives from American publishers because of the necessity of sharing earnings with publishers abroad.

Another important source of income for the songwriter is the money collected in his behalf by music performance rights societies. There are two major societies in the United States: the American Society of Composers, Authors and Publishers (ASCAP), and Broadcast Music, Inc. (BMI). They are basically licensing and collection agencies, and, though bitter competitors, together they control the public performance of virtually all copyrighted music in the United States.

The rights societies are founded on the premise, upheld by law, that if the creative endeavors of composers are used directly or indirectly to sell a product or to attract consumers, then the composers are entitled to share in the revenues. In the vernacular of the trade, this is called "getting a piece of the action." Therefore, on behalf of composers and their publishers, the rights organizations collect millions of dollars a year in fees from radio stations, television stations and networks, music installations in restaurants, cocktail lounges and retail stores; even airlines offering passengers recorded music must be licensed by the societies. Night clubs, theaters, concert halls — wherever "live" musical entertainment is offered — are subject to the control of the societies as well. From the revenues they collect, the societies deduct office rent, staff wages, taxes and other operating expenses before distributing the major portion among their memberships.

The distribution of money collected is based on the popularity of a member's music, and is calculated by means of an elaborate rating system. Both societies employ roving statisticians who periodically check the logs of radio and television stations to determine which tunes are being played most often. Juke boxes and "Muzak" installations are also surveyed. Periodically, the compiled data are fed back to headquarters, where they are used to establish ratings. The publishers and composers whose music is widely programmed are apt to receive fat checks, while those with low ratings may receive only a pittance.

Unlike songwriters, recording artists are not protected by any societies like ASCAP or BMI. A radio station that broadcasts a Simon and Garfunkel recording of a Paul Simon song must pay for the privilege of airing the song, but it is under no obligation to pay either member of the famous duo for the right to use his performance of it. And clearly the station is exploiting Simon and Garfunkel's rendition to maintain its audience ratings and thereby sell its sponsors' commercial products. A Senate subcommittee is currently investigating, at the behest of the recording industry, a proposal to alter the copyright laws to the extent that radio stations and juke box operators pay performance fees to recording artists and their firms. Such copyright laws exist in almost every other country in the western world, excluding the Communist Bloc nations. Naturally, the radio and juke box industries are violently opposed to the idea, claiming that higher operating costs would cause severe financial hardship. Radio executives argue that if the law went into effect they would have to adopt higher advertising rates with the result that many small advertisers would turn to less expensive media. They add that if the recording industry is, as has been reported in the press, still engaging in payola practices, it proves that radio's promotional contribution to the recording industry is invaluable, and should obviate the necessity of their paying for the right to air the records. Furthermore, they say that if recording companies have the money to spend on forcing radio play in the first place, they really don't need the additional income from performance fees.

The payola argument, at least, is specious. Not all record labels can afford to squander money on payola; and furthermore, it is radio station personnel themselves who are accepting the bribes. Obviously, some radio station owners still condone the practice.

It may be some time before performance copyrights are established by law, but to this writer it seems inevitable, when right is so clearly on the side of the recording industry and its artists.

Another legal problem that has affected the industry since its earliest days is piracy. It was only recently that Congress passed a law recognizing a recording company's ownership of the material contained on its master records and tapes. The new law does not place any restrictions on broadcasters with respect to the music they play over the air, but it does discourage tape and record pirates who flagrantly manufacture illegal copies of records and tapes and sell them at greatly reduced prices.

23

The Life Cycle of a Recording

FROM an economic standpoint, the long-playing album is the most important medium in the industry. Eighty-five percent of all records sold fall into this category.

On the other hand, the pop single has undergone a drastic change in status during the past few years. In the 1950s, it was the ultimate gauge of success in the industry. The walls in the offices of the top A&R men were lined with gold-plated, seven-inch discs, each symbolizing a recording that had sold a million copies. The more gold discs, the more powerful the man. But as the sales of long-playing records began to climb, the pop single began to be viewed in a different light. Although currently, pop single hits are still desirable, profitable and eagerly sought after, the truth is that the average pop single hit of today sells significantly fewer copies than it did ten years ago. There are several reasons for its decline. Today's public prefers its music on long-playing records or tape cartridges for obvious reasons: they provide more music for less money in the long run. But a much more serious problem for the pop single is the widespread and still growing practice among record fans of making tape copies of hit singles from borrowed records or radio broadcasts. Every copy taped is one fewer record the recording company will sell. Perhaps an equally important problem is the haste with which recording companies convert pop single hits to the more profitable long-play album format with its greater sales potential. Thus the life of the hit single is very short, indeed; but it does remain an invaluable promotional vehicle for new talent and album material.

In 1971, the Carpenters rocketed to fame on the wings of a superhit called "Close to You." However, it was a follow-up long-play album bearing the same title that actually brought the brother and sister team a tidy fortune, and at the same time enriched the coffers of A&M Records. On the other hand, in 1970 Columbia released a pop version of the then-new Simon and Garfunkel recording of "Bridge Over Troubled Waters" to promote the artists' latest album release of the same title. The incredible air play lavished on the single record by radio stations across the country pushed sales of the album well beyond the million mark in a matter of a few short weeks. The fact that the single record also sold over a million copies at the same time was a welcome, if unneeded, windfall.

Preparations for a recording session begin long before the featured artist or group sets foot in the studio for the "gig," as it is sometimes called. Studio time must be booked, engineers scheduled, orchestral arrangements commissioned and approved, musicians and singers hired and myriad other details attended to, including arranging for the cartage of heavy musical instruments to and from the recording studio, piano tuning, and so on. If a rock group is scheduled to record, the producer assigned to the job must sometimes be prepared to spend long hours in the studio control room, particularly if the group is one that creates its own musical material. It is a fairly well-known fact in the industry that many rock groups are notoriously slow workers in the studio environment. Often the members of a group are not able to anticipate how they will sound on tape. They must wait until the first takes of the session are played back. Should adjustments or even an entirely new approach be required as the group works together, the process can easily become long and arduous. Corrections or alternate themes very often cannot be simply jotted down and replayed by the performers; they must be memorized and rehearsed, sometimes for hours, before they are considered "right" for recording. Such emphasis on rehearsal and rote learning is often necessary because many rock musicians read music poorly or not at all.

The modern producer of recorded rock music must be conditioned not only to cope with this kind of expensive and time consuming exercise, he must also be expert at deploying musicians, tape channels, microphones and isolation panels within the walls of the studio to attain the best possible recorded sound and musical balance. Isolation panels are nearly soundproof, movable walls which the producer or audio engineer places between individual musicians or groups of musicians so that each can be recorded on individual tape channels. Sometimes the musicians have to wear headphones to enable them to hear each other. The wise producer strives for as much isolation as possible at rock sessions. It greatly simplifies the post-studio, or tape editing, phase of the production. For example, if a guitar player makes a mistake that goes undetected during a session, it will be a simple problem for the producer to correct as long as the mistake has been recorded only on the guitarist's track, or tape channel. The guitar player simply makes another recording of that particular passage later. If, however, the guitarist's mistake is picked up by the other microphones in the studio and thus recorded on other tape channels, it becomes necessary to rerecord that section of the music with the entire group.

Sessions organized for more orthodox stars — Andy Williams and Barbra Streisand are typical examples — are quite different and are more in the old tradition of the industry. Performers like these usually demand a creative studio force of thirty or forty musicians and a chorus of eight to twelve singers. These "side" musicians and singers must be expert performers with the ability to read music quickly and proficiently. They must also be masters of the difficult art of properly projecting instrumental or vocal sounds within the limited confines of a studio. But most important, they must be capable of executing these demanding tasks with little or no rehearsal.

Singers and musicians of such extraordinary caliber do exist. They are clustered, for the most part, around the country's leading recording centers, where their services are in constant demand.

The hiring of studio musicians and singers is conducted by union contractors employed by the producer. Since musicians and singers are represented by different unions, a contractor is required for each group. The conscientious contractor strives to assemble the available singers or musicians that will best suit the music to be recorded. He must be highly selective in his choice of personnel; a rock singer would not be a likely candidate for the chorus of *The Sound of Music.* The contractor must also perform several clerical chores at the session. He must see to it that union contract forms are completed and that his participating members file tax statements properly. Many contractors are themselves professional musicians or singers, and thus they may also perform at sessions. But the contractor's primary job is the recruitment of talent for the A&R man; and since contractors are paid rather handsomely for their work, double the pay scale of side musicians or singers, they usually go to considerable lengths to avoid hiring second-rate or inappropriate performers.

The large-scale popular recording session requires the services of yet another specialist, the arranger. It is a well-known fact that A&R men, artists and artist managers spend a great deal of time discussing the selection of musical material to be recorded. What is not as widely known is that they devote almost as much care to the choice of musical arrangers — the men or women who will compose the instrumental and vocal scores for the sessions. The average pop album requires the services of one to three arrangers.

The arranger has the imposing task of writing individual scores for each of the musicians or singers at a session with an end to placing the featured artist in the best possible musical setting. Top arrangers must be exceptionally skilled in musical composition and musicianship, as well as be adaptable to the constantly changing trends in popular music. The requirements and the standards are high, but so are the rewards. Not only does the arranger receive generous fees for his scores, he also conducts the studio orchestra in the performances of those scores, and for that he is paid at the same rate as the musicians' union contractor, about double the rate paid to a side musician. Arrangers whose services are constantly in demand often draw incomes of fifty thousand dollars a year.

It is not uncommon for A&R staff members employed by recording companies to double as arranger-conductors to augment their incomes. Most firms approve this practice, provided that the A&R men have a talent for writing commercially viable arrangements and, most important, that this activity does not detract from their regular duties, particularly supervision of recording sessions.

To better understand the role of the producer, or A&R man, let us assume that we are about to witness a recording session with a studio orchestra. To give a clear picture, we'll have our imagined producer be a conservative fellow who prefers to record on only four channels. (As many as sixteen would be available to him in most studios.) Except for a number of rock specialists, most producers aim to create the illusion of live sound on a recording. Therefore, the seating arrangement of the studio orchestra will often correspond to the seating arrangement of an orchestra on the concert stage or in the orchestra pit of a theater. In a four channel setup, our producer assigns three channels to the orchestra and the fourth to the vocalist or instrumental soloist. The first and second violinists will feed into the first, or left-hand, channel; the brass and woodwinds will occupy the second, or middle, channel; and the percussion and lower string instruments,

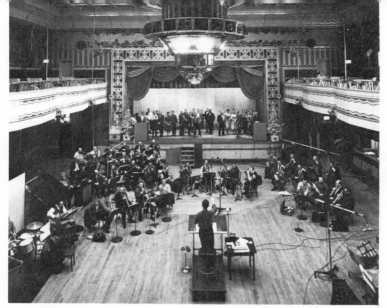

A modern, full-scale opera recording session

the basses and cellos, will feed into the third, or right-hand, channel. The fourth, or extra, channel is the province of the soloist, and it is brought to stage center later during the tape editing phase of the proceedings. The producer installs a separate microphone for each section of the studio orchestra; in addition, microphones are set up in front of a number of individual musicians within the orchestral sections. These so-called accent mikes are placed to record important instrumental solos or musical passages which the producer may want to have emphasized in the orchestral fabric. Several microphones are now feeding into each of the orchestral channels. Unlike the rock producer, who generally prefers to blend the instruments during tape editing, our orchestral producer will strive for "cross-feed" between the microphones. For example, the microphones located in the

215

woodwind section will pick up the sounds emanating from the brass, strings and percussion, and vice versa. This cross-feed heightens the illusion of sonic depth and orchestral spread. However, it must be delicately controlled to avoid throwing the orchestral sound out of balance.

Now let us assume that all of the creative and engineering forces are assembled and that the session is ready to get under way. The recording equipment has been thoroughly checked to make certain that all of the electronic components are functioning properly. The team includes two key members: one engineer to operate the tape recorders, and a second engineer — or "mixer" — to man the all-important "console," or control board.

The console is an imposing looking panel equipped with individual volume controls — called potentiometers, or "pots" — for up to thirty microphones. The more sophisticated consoles feature "submaster" pots which can command whole groups of microphones at a time. These controls make it possible to raise the sound levels of entire orchestral sections or large choral groupings as well as of individual musicians and singers.

Now the tape recorders are rolling; the producer, from his position behind the glass panel of the control room, signals the soloist and the conductor to begin, and the recording session is under way. As the session progresses, the producer directs the mixer's regulation of the sound intensities both of various sections of the orchestra and of individual instruments, according to the demands of the musical arrangement. The producer will also signal the mixer when accent mikes are to be opened or closed. The mixer must react quickly and unerringly to the producer's

*A modern console. The "mixer" pictured here has sixteen
tape channels at his disposal*

instructions. Mistakes are costly. Should the sound picked
up by two or three microphones be recorded on a single
tape channel in the wrong balance, there is no way to
correct the error short of rerecording the entire passage.
Thus, the mixer plays a vitally important role in the realization of the producer's recording plans.

However, the mixer has other important chores to perform besides the execution of the producer's commands.
The mixer is also responsible for monitoring the intensities of the sounds being fed to the tape channels. If the
signals from the microphones are recorded at low levels,

there is the possibility that the master tape will be plagued by a poor signal-to-noise ratio, and that tape hiss and other extraneous noises will be noticeable on the final record pressings and prerecorded tape cartridges. On the other hand, too great a sound intensity will cause distortion and create stylus tracking problems. An extremely loud passage, especially in the bass registers, can actually pop a needle out of a record groove. The mixer does not rely solely on his ears to control the sound levels being generated by the various open microphones. The console has what are called VU (volume unit) meters that register continuous measurement of the sounds produced by each individual microphone.

As the session progresses, technical problems present themselves constantly, but the producer must, nevertheless, focus most of his attention on the artistic effect of the recording. The producer alone is expected to judge whether the featured artist and the side musicians and singers are performing at the peak of their capabilities. When the producer becomes dissatisfied with the way the music is being performed or interpreted, he calls a halt to the proceedings and asks that the performance be repeated, often suggesting changes in approach. Each repeat performance of a given selection is called a "take." Like most A&R directors, our producer is a stickler for quality, requiring several "takes" of each song before he is completely satisfied. He even goes one step further, asking the artist to rerecord small sections of each song. These are called "inserts."

Three hours later our session comes to an end. Because of performing union regulations, of all of the music recorded during one session, only fifteen minutes may be extracted and used on the end products — records and tape cartridges. Usually two to three sessions are required for an LP. Once the work of the singers and musicians is completed, the producer must begin a whole new round of activities, starting with the tape editing phase of the operation.

During the editing stage of a long-play album, the producer selects the best takes from his tapes and arranges them in the sequence in which they will appear on the record and tape labels. The next step is to "equalize" the chosen takes, a process of lowering or raising sound levels, and of brightening or softening recorded passages, so that all of the selections, when heard as a group, are homogeneous. Finally, the four individual channels utilized at the session must be combined to make two before they can be transferred to stereo discs and tape cartridges. To maintain the illusion of stereo sound, the original middle channel must be divided equally between the final left- and right-hand channels; so must the fourth channel, the one containing the recorded sounds of the featured artist. This is accomplished by electronic wizardry too complicated for us to consider in these pages. Suffice it to say that to the listener in his living room, the featured artist will seem to be right in the middle of the orchestra on an illusionary audio stage center.

When the editing work is done, the sounds contained on the final dual-track tape will be transferred, in the form of grooves, by a record-cutting lathe onto the surface of a disc. The disc is made of acetate, hence its name in the industry is "reference acetate." From the cutting lathe, the reference acetate is sent directly to the

A tape editing session

A mastering cubicle. The cutting lathe is shown on the left

producer. After listening to it carefully, the producer may elect to do more editing. Indeed, a number of acetates may be cut before the producer is satisfied enough to give his final stamp of approval. The fully approved and edited tape copy is now the "master tape," from which a final reference acetate is made.

Our record album is now ready for manufacture and sale. However, there may be further delays before it is released to the public. The marketing wing of the recording company may decide to postpone its issue until the record-buying season is at its peak, or until promotional plans are formulated. During the period between its completion and its formal release, the album is consigned to a kind of limbo called "the icebox."

Finally, the announcement of the release date of the album triggers a whole new round of activity within the company. Responsibility for the album is transferred from the A&R staff to the marketing division of the company. The transition takes place formally at a joint A&R and marketing meeting, which is held monthly in most recording firms. The purpose of these meetings is to plan sales and promotional strategies for albums and single records scheduled for release three or four months in the future. Our producer — he will usually be one of several producers attending the meeting — will play portions of the album for the marketing specialists (sales, promotion and advertising managers, the publicity director, the art director, and the people who write and edit the notes printed on record and tape jackets); and he will convey to them what, in his opinion, the commercial potential of the album is, and for what sort of audience the album will have its greatest appeal.

If our producer's record has obvious teen-age appeal, the publicity director will prepare stories and news items about the artist who performs on the album for magazines and periodicals catering to the youth market. The promotion manager will schedule appearances for the artist on radio disc jockey shows. The art director will set about designing a jacket cover that will enhance the artist's image and attract attention in record shops. The advertising manager will map plans to include the album in printed advertisements and paid radio commercials sponsored by the recording company. Other specialists in the sales department will provide the manufacturing division with sales projections for the album, so that quantities can be determined for ordering record pressings, jackets and tape cartridges. Estimating sales for established recording stars is usually a simple matter; figuring out what a new artist will sell is almost always guesswork.

While the marketing staff is busily at work creating a demand for our artist, the album goes through the final stage of its development prior to release: the manufacturing operation.

The manufacturing process begins with the preparation of the lacquer, a special disc made by the cutting lathe operator from the master tape. Next, the lacquer is forwarded by the engineering department directly to the pressing plant. Here the disc is carefully cleaned and washed before it is sprayed with a silver nitrate solution. The surface of the lacquer is then covered with a thin, electrically conductible coating of silver. Next, the silvered lacquer is placed in a plating bath where, after undergoing an electrochemical process, a copper shell is fused to its surface. The copper shell is stripped from the

Stripping the silvered lacquer from the reference lacquer

lacquer, bringing with it the lacquer's silver coating. This copper shell, with the silver fused to its surface, is called the "master." Since the grooves on the surface of the master are the reverse of those on the lacquer, it is a "negative" which cannot be played. The master reenters the baths to produce "mothers," positive metal discs that *can* be played. In turn, the mothers are placed in the baths to form "stampers." Additional coatings of copper and chromium are applied to the surfaces of the stampers to render them extremely hard and durable. The stamp-

A record press in operation

ers, being the exact reverse of the mothers, are negatives.

The next step in the process is the forwarding of the finished stampers to the press room, where they are placed in the record presses.

The record press resembles a huge waffle iron, and functions somewhat like one. The upper and lower jaws of the press are called mold blocks. The stampers are fixed in the mold blocks, one for each side of the record. A square biscuit made of vinylite, a soft plastic compound, is sandwiched between two round paper labels that bear the names of the record, artist, and musical selections on the albums. This sandwich is placed on the spindle of the press. The jaws of the press are subsequently closed under great hydraulic pressure and extremely hot steam is pumped through the mold blocks. The enormous pressure coupled with the intense heat generated by the steam causes the vinylite biscuit to melt and spread evenly over the negative grooves of the stampers. As soon as the melting cycle is completed, cold water is forced through pipes located in the mold blocks. The cooling cycle hardens the biscuit, now in the form of a flat, grooved disc. The disc is a positive, the reverse of the stamper, so that now we have a record ready for market. The time consumed by the pressing operation has been only forty seconds.

Should a hundred thousand or more pressings of an individual album be required, ten or more presses will be reserved for the production run. It will also be necessary for the plant's plating department to produce many sets of stampers, since they do wear out with use. This can happen after a set of stampers has produced a thousand pressings, or as few as a hundred, depending upon how they bear up under the heat and pressure of the press. It is the responsibility of the quality control department to determine when stampers are no longer fit for use. This is accomplished by simply taking one record from a batch turned out by a given set of stampers and listening to it. If the sound of the record shows signs of deterioration, the stampers are immediately removed from the press

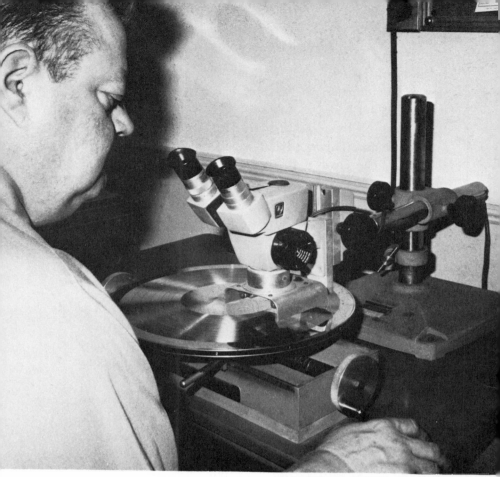

Examining a master disc for possible flaws

and a fresh set is installed. The ratio of records manufactured to those tested for quality varies from record plant to record plant. The more quality-conscious record makers test one record in every hundred produced.

If many sets of stampers are required, as in the case of a hit album or single, it becomes necessary for the plating department to make additional masters and mothers. And since mothers and masters also deteriorate with age and frequent use, the complete cycle from master tape to stamper will be repeated many times over in the life of a successful, active recording.

The pressings of our album are now stacked on spindles and transferred from the press room to the collating room. Here they are inserted into protective inner sleeves and their illustrated jackets, and then they are run through a special machine that wraps and seals them in transparent plastic sheaths. The finished albums are then packed in cartons and forwarded to the plant's warehouse to await shipment.

Let's imagine that our album has also been scheduled for release in the eight-track stereo tape cartridge and cassette formats. In that case, parallel manufacturing activities have been taking place at the tape duplicating plant. The first step in the process is to make a narrow-gauge eight-track copy and a cassette copy of the original dual track, a 15-inches-per-second master tape approved by the producer. The eight-track copy is called a sub-master, and plays at a speed of 3¾ inches per second. The cassette copy is called the running master, and plays at a speed of 1⅞ inches per second. The sound from the sub-master tape and the cassette running master is copied onto duplicate eight-track tapes and cassettes on a series of "slave" tape machines linked to the master tape recorders. This duplicating operation is conducted at a very high speed.

The final phase of the life cycle of our album is its distribution and sale. Meanwhile, the marketing force has been hard at work attempting to promote our artist's recordings through radio and television exposure, news-

Record albums crated and ready for shipment

paper and magazine advertising, and in-store and window displays at record shops. By now, it is hoped, the
public knows that the album exists and has heard a sam-
pling of the recorded material on the radio.

Today the business of getting albums to the people who
want to buy them is fairly complicated. It was not always
so. Two decades ago a recording company sold its prod-

ucts to a group of regional distributors. Each distributor held an exclusive franchise to sell the manufacturer's products to the retail stores in his territory. Record distributing organizations and retail stores specializing in the sale of records and tapes continue to play extremely important roles in the marketing of sound products in the United States, but they have been joined by several new channels to the record buyer over the past twenty years: record clubs, one-stops, rack jobbers and premium merchants.

A record club is a familiar and popular way for recording fans to obtain records and tapes at considerable savings. However, clubs do have their drawbacks: members are limited to the selection of material offered by a club; and writing to a computer to correct mistakes can be a frustrating and nerve-racking experience. Before joining a club, the prospective member would be wise to read all of the fine print in the club's advertisement. He or she should also determine the actual cost of the records or tapes to be received from the club for comparison with local retail store prices. This can be done by totaling all mailing and handling charges and the cost of the records or tapes the member is committed to buy during the term of the agreement stated on the advertisement's return coupon, then dividing by the total number of records or tapes the member will receive, including bonus selections. This arithmetic will give the prospective member the average unit cost of each recording offered by the club.

The one-stop is the oldest of the additions to the industry's basic marketing channels. The term simply means a center where the inventories of all major record labels and many smaller ones are available to the buyer; hence, he only has to make "one stop." Originally the function of the one-stop was to provide service to juke box operators who had grown weary of making the rounds to as many as twenty different local record distributors to obtain the replacement records they needed for their machines. Then the one-stop became the place where the operator could buy all current hits and potential new hits — regardless of label. Not only did the one-stop save the operator time, it cut his traveling expenses. But the operator paid — and still pays, for that matter — a higher price for the convenience, as the one-stop in turn must buy its records from the local distributors. One-stop trade used to be confined almost exclusively to pop singles, but in recent years it has expanded into the popular and classical album business, as increasing numbers of small retail stores have begun to avail themselves of this convenient method of obtaining merchandise.

Without doubt the most powerful and influential merchants in the industry are the rack jobbers, or subdistributors, as they are sometimes called. At one time rack jobbers specialized in servicing record rack installations in supermarkets, drugstores and other types of retail businesses not specifically devoted to record sales. But as rack jobbing matured it became more sophisticated, and the simple record rack metamorphosed into a full-fledged department offering thousands of selections on both disc and tape. Many rack jobbers also manage, or "program," neighborhood record shops. Under this arrangement the rack jobber furnishes the shop with all of the merchandise it needs for stock, and agrees to constantly replace slow moving or unsalable titles with selections that presumably will sell well. He or she also does the buying and servic-

The record department of the Harvard Cooperative Society in Cambridge, Massachusetts, one of the largest retail outlets for recordings in the world

ing, and assumes most of the risks, while the shop owner provides the space and pays the rent. Although there are many different kinds of "program" arrangements, the rack jobber is basically a concessionaire who pays the retail store owner a percentage of the revenues derived from the sale of records and tapes. The retailer makes a smaller profit than he would if he did his own buying and maintained his own inventory of merchandise, but on the other hand, he need not make major investments in record stock.

It does not take a marketing expert to see that giant

rack jobbing establishments in control of hundreds of retail outlets can wield enormous power — power that most big rack jobbers are not reluctant to exercise. They put constant pressure on manufacturers to sell at lower prices in exchange for the "quantity buy." All too often a recording company suffering a cold spell on the market will capitulate.

It is also standard industry practice for manufacturers to grant their distributors an extra 10 percent discount on all of the business the distributors transact with rack jobbers. The discount is passed on to the rack jobber, presumably for the special service he renders. But a number of independent retailers consider the discount to be discriminatory.

The price squeeze is not the only pressure brought to bear by the giant rack jobbers on the recording companies. Frequently jobbers return thousands and even hundreds of thousands of unsold records to the companies for full credit. Furthermore, they tend to buy only the safe or sure-fire recording titles listed on the trade's various best-seller charts. This conservatism on the part of jobbers is understandable, considering that they furnish merchandise to hundreds of different retail outlets on a guaranteed basis. This means that the retailers can return unsold records for full credit. Under such circumstances, it would be poor business practice to supply these outlets with untried recordings. Even the most careful professional buyer, whether employed by a giant rack establishment or a small retail shop, can wind up with a stock of "dead," or unsalable, records and tapes through no fault of his own.

A case in point was the abrupt end of the Mitch Miller

"Sing Along" about a decade and a half ago. Sales of Miller's choral albums — which were collections of fresh arrangements of old chestnuts like "There's A Long, Long Trail A'Winding," "Sweet Adeline," "For Me And My Gal" and "My Gal Sal" — had flourished for several years. But the day suddenly arrived when the public seemed to decide that it had had quite enough of Mr. Miller and his Gang. The boom turned into a bust almost as rapidly as a pin bursts a balloon, leaving Columbia Records' distribution pipelines clogged with millions of newly manufactured Mitch Miller albums. In this case, Columbia was forced to absorb, or "eat" as they say in the trade, virtually all of the unsold "Sing Along" albums then in circulation; this probably cost the company a large portion of the profits it had enjoyed from the Mitch Miller boom.

The conservatism of the rack jobbing establishment poses severe problems for small labels attempting to get more retail exposure, or for any label wanting to promote recordings of specialized interest or recordings by new, relatively unknown artists or groups. More than half of all of the records and tapes sold in this country pass through the hands of rack merchants. Thus, the rack jobbing establishment possesses the clout to jeopardize the existence of any label, regardless of size, particularly when the label suffers a long hitless dry spell. During such a spell, a recording company must rely on the sales of the staple items in its catalogue for survival. But rack jobbers are notoriously poor purveyors of catalogue material for the simple reason that current hits sell faster and are less risky than yesterday's best sellers. Then what does a large label do to ensure distribution for its catalogue? It enters the rack jobbing or retail business itself; several leading companies have done so in recent years.

Before we leave the subject of distribution, it might be worthwhile to briefly outline the price structure of the industry. Naturally, pricing in a business as volatile as the recording trade is always subject to wide variances; but some sort of standards must prevail from which the variances are made. Of course, there are also industry norms dictated by economics and tradition. Typically, a record store buys its wares from distributors at 38 percent off the suggested retail list prices established by manufacturers. According to this formula, an album with a list price of $4.98 should cost the dealer $3.09. Distributors in turn buy from the manufacturers they represent at a discount of 55 percent off retail list prices. At this rate, a $4.98 album would cost the distributor $2.24. Thus, the dealer who sells the album at full list price will realize a profit of $1.89, while the distributor's unit profit, based on the dealer cost of $3.09, is $.85. Theoretically, the distributor works on a smaller profit margin than the retailer because of the greater volume of business the distributor transacts. But actually, most manufacturers, distributors and dealers operate on even lower profit margins than those outlined above. This is because of the highly competitive nature of the business and the rampant and widespread practice of discounting records and tape cartridges in retail stores across the country.

Perhaps the most extreme form of discounting — one apparently condoned by the leading recording companies — is the record and tape package offer that is advertised on television so often. To be in a position to sell even old recordings at such attractive prices — four long-playing records of past hits for $6.98 is a typical offer — the recording company or the independent entrepreneur sponsoring the TV commercial must first haggle to procure special copyright rates for the music contained in the multirecord and tape packages. The TV bonanza, with its potential of hundreds of thousands of sales, especially of older recorded material, has led many publishers to cut their regular prices by half or even by three-quarters.

Few recording artists can stand in the way of this form of discounting, since virtually all artist contracts give the manufacturer the sole right to establish the selling prices of the artist's records and tapes. Only those artists who have noncoupling clauses in their recording contracts present a problem to the manufacturer; such clauses prohibit the manufacturer from combining the artist's recorded performances with those of other artists in albums without the artist's specific consent. However, the promise of extra income derived from their older recordings and from free television plugs has prompted most artists to agree to the special record and tape package offers.

Another form of drastic discounting is the fairly common use of recordings as premiums. Commercial companies generally offer people premiums either to induce them to take action or to encourage them to buy a specific product. Thus tire companies offer new Christmas records for sale at the height of the gift-buying season to stimulate customer traffic at their retail locations, and breakfast food companies at times offer records in exchange for a required number of box tops.

Some observers of the recording scene deplore television and premium offers with the view that these schemes will eventually destroy the industry's catalogue trade, the public's confidence in the integrity of recording companies, and the values they place on their products in retail outlets. Why, for example, should a record produced and manufactured by Columbia Records cost only $1.75 if purchased via television, when other records produced by the company cost twice as much on retail counters, even after deducting discounts? One of the most important reasons is that by dealing directly with the customer, the company does not have to build in profits for the distributor or the record dealer in its price structure. Although the explanation is accurate, it is not obvious to the vast majority of record fans.

The marketing head of a recording firm, particularly a large one, must keep all of the channels for distributing records and tapes — rack jobbers, one-stops, distributors, retail shops, record clubs, premium channels or television offers — in the proper perspective and balance. He must utilize all of them to the best possible advantage, without permitting any one of them to jeopardize his company's image or financial success. He must simultaneously oversee the activities and the planning of his firm's sales, merchandising and promotion specialists. As if these responsibilities were not imposing enough, the chief marketing executive must also keep a sharp eye on any new developments in the marketplace, in both the technical and artistic fields. Any news, or even rumors, of technical advances must be reported to his management promptly. The recording company that fails to react quickly to innovations in recording techniques may find itself in a seriously weakened position in the industry if the public embraces the new trends.

The Life Cycle of a Recording

Procrastination can prove very costly. Back in the late fifties a number of important companies remained unconvinced that stereo records would become a popular home entertainment medium; they continued to record highly expensive classical repertoire in monaural only. Soon the public refused to buy any recording without a stereo label, and the companies were forced to rerecord the same repertoire in stereo at considerable additional expense. Quad sound has created a similar dilemma for contemporary recording executives.

The marketing chief must report to his superiors and peers the successes and failures of his company's recordings, as well as those of his competitors, realistically. If there are strong indications that a new recording trend is in the offing, this fact must be conveyed to the label's A&R staffers so that they can "get with it." If a current musical craze or a popular artist on the company's roster is waning in popularity, this fact must be made known to the management so that further contract commitments to the artists riding the craze can be deferred or eliminated altogether.

These are serious responsibilities in a constantly changing industry, so full of risks and worries. But there do appear to be some healthy signs for the future. Currently there seems to be a strong trend away from the rack jobber managed retail outlet, which promotes only hit records and tapes with a sprinkling of bargain priced hits from previous years. A group of new retail chain stores have sprouted up around the country. These stores offer a wide variety of recorded fare, ranging in scope from the songs of Elton John to Elizabethan madrigals. If this development continues, it will be a boon to the serious recording fan who has found it difficult to satisfy his needs at local retail establishments, and it will prove that the public's taste in music is broader than most recording executives have yet realized. Many of the young fans that cut their teeth on the Beatles have become enthusiastic supporters of such highly sophisticated groups as the Yes and Emerson, Lake and Palmer, groups that rely heavily on the music of Bach, Brahms, Copland and Moussorgsky for inspiration. Perhaps the new trend will continue to point to an underlying unity in music, as the wall between pops and classics grows thinner.

But whatever the future holds for the record industry, someone will be on the scene with a microphone and a tape recorder to capture it in sound. Others will be on hand to package it in some form; still others will deliver it to the customers who wish to buy it. Although the record business is in a constant state of flux, its tasks will never change in essence — at least as long as the public insists on hearing the music it wants to hear *when* it wants to hear it.

Index

239

Index

242

Index

Owen, William Barry, 48, 49–50, 58, 63

Paar, Jack, 159
Page, Anita, 88
Page, Patti, 143
Paley, William S., 104, 105, 123
Paramount Records, 178, 196
Parker, Tom, 191
Pathé Brothers, 47, 50, 75, 83
Payne, Colonel, 20, 21, 22, 23, 35
payola, 139–42, 207–08
performance fee, 138–39; for artists, 207–08; for composers, 206–07
performance rights societies, 206–07
Petrillo, James, 109–10, 111
Philadelphia Orchestra, 84, 106, 192
Philco, 120, 123, 124
Philips Records, 169, 173
phonautograph, 6–7, 40
phonogram, 8, 11, 12, 17, 19
phonograph, 13–15, 34, 40, 44, 48, 54n; invention of, 3, 7–8; demonstrations of, 4–5, 10; structure and operation of, 8–9; promotion of, 11–12; as dictating machine, 18, 23, 41; improvements of, 18–19, 35, 44, 45, 51, 69; marketing of, 22; coin-operated, 25–27, 45, 47
Pinocchio, 89, 103
piracy, 32–33, 51–52, 208
Platters, the, 143
pop single, 201–02, 209–10
popular recordings, 187; of 1930s, 101, 105–06; of 1940s, 112; of 1950s, 143, 145–46, 159; of 1960s, 159, 164, 191; of 1970s, 210
Porter, Cole, 160
Porter, Steve, 47
Poulsen, Valdemar, 116
Prescott, F. M., 65
Presley, Elvis, 145, 191
Prima, Louis, 101

quadrasonic sound, 166–68
Quinn, Dan, 45, 47, 55

rack jobber, 229, 230–34, 237
radio, and record industry, 79–81, 86, 95, 102, 109, 138–42, 176–77, 207–08
Radio Corporation of America, 86, 87, 92, 119
Radiola, 86
radio programs, of 1940s, 137
RCA Victor, 88, 89, 93–94, 95, 96, 97, 101, 102, 104, 106, 107, 111, 119–21, 122, 123, 123n, 124, 125, 126–27, 129, 173, 186, 191, 192, 195
Read, Oliver, 86
record. *See* cylinder, prerecorded; disc, prerecorded; long-playing records
record changer, 123, 127
record chart, 101, 140
record club, 229
record company: structure of, 180–89; means of acquiring artists, 190–98
record industry, 174–77; and invention of phonograph, 3, 7–8; and invention of graphophone, 16; and invention of gramophone, 41; abroad, 47, 48, 75, 76, 93; golden age of, 65, 71–78, 79–90; and trends in music, 76–78, 105–06, 145–46; and radio, 79–81, 86, 95, 102, 109, 138–42, 176–77, 207–08; and movies, 88–90, 100, 102–04, 196; and 1929 crash, 91–98; renaissance of, 99–112; and development of tape recorder, 115; and development of long-playing record, 119–30; and growth of independent labels, 131–32; retailing and distribution methods of, 132–33, 177–78, 197, 227–35; and development of high-fidelity record, 133–35; scandals within, 139–42; and development of stereophonic record, 147, 149, 150–51; and development of quadrasonic record, 166, 167; projected future developments in, 169–70; marketing methods of, 186, 221–22;

244

Index

Index

Taft, William Howard, 69
Tainter, Charles Sumner, 16, 17, 18, 19, 20
Tainter-Bell patents, 18, 20, 21, 35, 36, 52, 53, 54, 61
talking recordings, early, 29, 45, 47, 69
tape, magnetic, 118, 151–54, 227; multitrack, 211–12, 155–58; pre-recorded, 151–54, 227
tape cartridge, eight-track stereo-phonic, 152–53, 227
tape cassette, stereophonic, 152, 153–54, 227
tape deck, stereophonic, 151–52
tape recorder, 115–18
Tate, Alfred O., 16
Teldec, 169, 185
Telegraphone, 116
television, record offers on, 233–34, 235–36
Thomas A. Edison Company, 91–92
Tijuana Brass, 175, 176
Tilton, Martha, 112
Time magazine, 141, 142
Tin Pan Alley, 74, 102, 138
Tommy, 198
tone arm, 60, 120
Top Hit Playlist, 140–41
Toscanini, Arturo, 101
Tracey, Arthur, 98
Tucker, Sophie, 90
Twain, Mark, 47
2001, 196

United States Copyright Office, 204
United States Gramophone Com-pany, 42, 52
United States Marine Band, 27, 28

Vallee, Rudy, 86, 90, 109
Vanguard Records, 131
Variety, 101
Vaughn, Sarah, 143

Victor Records, 57–58, 63, 64
Victor Talking Machine Company, 57, 60, 62, 69, 71, 74, 75, 76, 77, 78, 80–81, 83, 84, 86–87, 92
Victrola, 65–67, 69, 75
Vitaphone, 53
Vocalian Records, 75
Vox Records, 127, 131

Wagon Master, The, 89
Wallerstein, Edward, 95–96, 104, 105, 106, 107, 111, 119, 120–21, 122, 123, 123n, 124, 127, 129
Wallichs, Glenn, 108
Ward, Helen, 112
Waring, Fred, 78, 109
Warner Brothers, 88, 92–93, 97, 173
Watch Your Step, 76
Waters, Ethel, 89
Webb, Jimmy, 161
Welch, Walter L., 86
Western Electric Company, 83, 84
Westminster Records, 131
West Side Story, 145, 194
We Take the Town, 195
Wexler, Jerry, 176
Whiteman, Paul, 78, 80
Who, the, 162, 193, 198
Williams, Andy, 190, 191–92, 212
Williams, Roger, 143
Winter, Johnny, 192
Wizard of Oz, The, 104
World War I, and record industry, 74, 75, 76, 78
World War II, and record indus-try, 107–08, 111, 133
Wynn, Ed, 109, 137
Wynshaw, David, 142

Yes, the, 162, 238

Zonophone, 53, 54, 61, 62